TIMING

TIMING

by Alistair McGowan

From an idea by Paul Dornan and Alistair McGowan

JOSEF WEINBERGER PLAYS

LONDON

TIMING
First published in 2009
by Josef Weinberger Ltd
12-14 Mortimer Street, London, W1T 3JJ
www.josef-weinberger.com
general.info@jwmail.co.uk

The author asserts his moral right to be identified as the author of the work.

ISBN 978 0 85676 331 1

Printed in England by Commercial Colour Press plc, Hainault, Essex.

TIMING was first produced by Nica Burns and Max Weitzenhoffer at the King's Head Theatre, London, on 30th September 2009, with the following cast:

JULIAN	Edward Baker-Duly
PHIL	Paul Bazely
PRESTON	Matt Cross
LEONIE	Louise Ford
DINO	Dean Gaffney
WES	Peter Hamilton Dyer
AMANDA	Georgia Mackenzie

Directed by Tamara Harvey
Designed by Lucy Osborne
Lighting designed by Oliver Fenwick
Sound designed by Emma Laxton
Costume Supervisor Sydney Florence
Associate Producer Tara Hull

CHARACTERS

PHIL, 42, sound engineer

PRESTON, 21, trainee engineer/studio dogsbody/runner

LEONIE, 23, Producer

JULIAN, 39, voice-over artist

WES, 37, advertising copywriter

DINO, 32, advertising copywriter

AMANDA, 35, actress and voice-over artist

ACKNOWLEDGEMENTS

For taking part in pre-performance readings of the play I would like to thank Tobias Beer, Dom Colchester, Scarlett Strallen, Lisa Thorner, Matt Cross, Paul Chahidi, John Ramm, Sara Stewart, Ian Conningham.

And: Samantha Bond, Aden Gillett, Alex Hanson, Paul Thornley.

For helping to stage those reading, warm thanks to Nica Burns, David Babani and Tom Siracusa, Alix Harvey–Thompson, Brendan O'Hea and James Minihane.

For all their comments and input: Terry Johnson, Nica Burns, Tamara Harvey and the cast.

And for all their support: Alan Brodie and Harriet Pennington Legh

And for helping to turn a vague idea into a story, Paul Dornan.

THE SETTING

A voice-over studio, in London. Lunchtime. To the right of the stage (stage left) is the small, intimate booth, mikes suspended above two chairs, half-finished bottles of water and old scripts left out. The stage (and the studio) is divided by a piece of soundproof glass – which we don't need to see.

On the other side of the 'glass' (stage right) is the mixing desk and behind the desk is the chair, on wheels, of the engineer, PHIL. He has room to move around behind his chair on the wooden floor. There is then a carpeted area in which are two very large sofas at ninety degrees, separated by a table on which lie a number of very neat, very trendy magazines and executive toys, a fruit bowl and jars of miniature chocolates. There are two phones, one on PHIL'S desk and one in between the sofas. There are also two 'talkback' buttons to enable the 'creatives' to talk to the 'voices' – one next to PHIL, one in/on the table between the sofas.

Upstage are two doors in thick pine which lead out of the studio and the booth into the corridor behind. They both have little, round portal windows. There are three large windows at the back of the set: two on the creatives' side and one in the booth – they are both covered by thin-Slatted, Venetian blinds which are down but not closed.

N.B. When the dialogue starts to intertwine, the non-speaking half of the stage never freezes. The gaps are played as pauses – the characters trying to find the right words.

References to TV names may be updated (within reason) to suit whoever is current, however the author's permission must be sought. Please contact Josef Weinberger Plays for more information.

*As the lights come up, we hear the sound of 'tone' – a long,
loud piercing noise like the noise TVs used to make when the
transmission ended. This lasts for five seconds before*
PRESTON, *the young runner enters. He tidies up the studio and
then goes next door to tidy up the booth from the previous
session, picking up scripts and water bottles, pencils and
coffee mugs, sweet wrappers, etc. As* PRESTON *is in the booth,*
PHIL *enters the studio. He hits a button on his desk and the
tone goes off.* PRESTON *returns to the studio.*

PRESTON	'The Voice' is here.
PHIL	(*correcting*) It's 'Voice-over artist'.
PRESTON	Know what I mean.
PHIL	Who is it?
PRESTON	Julian Mann.
PHIL	Oh, nice! Haven't seen Julian for months.
PRESTON	He's on the phone, innit?
PHIL	Our phone or his mobile?
PRESTON	Our phone.
PHIL	Talk about looking after the pennies . . .
PRESTON	And Leonie's out there too, man. Looking sweet.
PHIL	(*ironic*) Ah! The lovely Leonie! Such a talent.
PRESTON	I thought you said she didn't know nothing about directing actors . . .
PHIL	(*disingenuously*) I'm sure I didn't.
PRESTON	And wouldn't know a good script if it went down on her . . .
PHIL	But when you went to Cambridge and your uncle runs the company . . .
PRESTON	And you've got great legs . . .

PHIL   Job for life.

PRESTON   I went to Cambridge, innit?

PHIL   What?

PRESTON   Last weekend.

PHIL   Oh!

PRESTON   All them bikes, man! It was like that Tour of de
            France – without the drugs!

PHIL   Or not!

PRESTON   True dat. D'you think I could get a date with
            Leonie?

PHIL   (*breath*) No.

PRESTON   You're doubting me?

PHIL   Well, she was pretty 'out of it' last night – as the
            young people say.

PRESTON   Maybe I'll get to go to one of them 'do's' some
            time.

            (PHIL *doesn't answer.*)

PRESTON   Are they heavy?

PHIL   What?

PRESTON   Are they safe?

PHIL   What?

PRESTON   Are they 'fun'?

PHIL   Oh. (*Pause.*) No.

PRESTON   But I'll bet there's loads of well nice women there,
            yeah?

PHIL   Yes.

PRESTON	Oh, man! Heavy! Know what I mean?
PHIL	Not often. (*A pause.*)
PRESTON	Shall I send them in?
PHIL	Yeah. Let's do it!
PRESTON	'nother coffee, Phil?
PHIL	No, thanks. If I have another coffee, I'll . . . do . . . something silly.
PRESTON	Like tell Leonie how gorgeous she is?
PHIL	No.
PRESTON	Know what I mean.

(PRESTON *leaves the room.* PHIL *fiddles with some of the hundreds of buttons and sliders on his sound desk.*)

PHIL	No. I don't know what you mean. And I don't know why you don't wear trousers that fit and I don't know what you see in . . .

(LEONIE *enters.*)

PHIL	. . . Leonie!
LEONIE	Hi, Paul!
PHIL	Phil.
LEONIE	Phil! Sorry! How are you? I haven't seen you for ages!
PHIL	Apart from last night.
LEONIE	Were you at the awards?
PHIL	Yeah. You said 'Hello'.
LEONIE	Did I?

PHIL   Yes. 'Hello, Pete,' you said.

LEONIE   No! I think I was a bit out of it!

PHIL   Really?

LEONIE   Yeah. We all went for beers before at *Miso's* and then there was the champagne reception and they just kept pouring this wine all through the meal. It was like . . .

PHIL   . . . being at work?

LEONIE   Yeah! No! I never drink at work. Not since . . . yeah, hm . . . Och, wasn't that beef just awful!

PHIL   I had the vegetarian option.

LEONIE   You a veggie then?

PHIL   No.

LEONIE   Oh. (*Beat.*) Jonathan Ross was great though, wasn't he?

PHIL   Very good. Much better than Chris Moyles. So quick!

LEONIE   And so rude! I thought I was going to wet myself!

PHIL   I'm sure that would have made Jonathan's night.

LEONIE   I nearly wet myself when Sean Bean went up for that award too!

PHIL   Perhaps you should see a doctor.

LEONIE   He's been brilliant for *O2!*

PHIL   It could be cystitis.

LEONIE   'See what you can do!' I'd like to see what I could do with you, Sean Bean! I honestly nearly lost it when I saw him!

PHIL   You could be pregnant!

LEONIE	I think I'm pretty safe on that score, thank you, Paul!
PHIL	Phil.
PRESTON	(*entering*) It's Julian!
	(PRESTON *enters with* JULIAN MANN. JULIAN *carries a newspaper and a mobile phone.*)
LEONIE	What? Oh, hi! Are you the voice?
JULIAN	'Voice-over artist'. Yes ...
LEONIE	Sorry, I must stop doing that; terrible habit.
JULIAN	(*playful*) Terrible.
PRESTON	(*to* LEONIE) I always do that.
PHIL	How are you, matey?
JULIAN	Fine. Thanks, matey. How're you?
PHIL	Good! Busy.
JULIAN	That's how we like it! How are the kids?
PHIL	Great. Really.
JULIAN	Good.
PHIL	Yeah, at a very nice age.
JULIAN	Terrific.
PHIL	Just out of that awful whining phase and starting to ask questions about everything.
JULIAN	Excellent.
PHIL	It's so rewarding, you know, seeing a little version of yourself running around and ...

JULIAN   Yeah. That's really nice. (*A short awkward silence.*) You are expecting me?

LEONIE   Yes! Sorry. Leonie – from MBSTWD and D . . .

JULIAN   Hi! It's just that my agent said it was a 'heavy pencil' for today, then I never actually heard back but I've just had an eleven o'clock over at *Sugar*, so I thought I'd pop in. And Kirsty, on the desk, said you were . . .

LEONIE   We *are* expecting you.

JULIAN   Good!

PRESTON   Can I get you a drink, Julian, yeah?

JULIAN   Thanks, Preston. Yes. An Earl Grey tea, please.

PRESTON   Milk and one sugar, innit.

JULIAN   (*impressed*) It is. I'll go through.

            (JULIAN *leaves for the booth.*)

PRESTON   Anything for you, Leonie?

LEONIE   Can I have a coffee, please?

PRESTON   Yeah, man.

LEONIE   Do you have decaf?

PRESTON   Yep. You want milk, 'n' that?

LEONIE   Is it semi-skimmed milk?

PRESTON   No. We've only got the full fat, 'n' that.

LEONIE   Oh. Okay.

            (PRESTON *starts to leave.* JULIAN *enters the booth.*)

LEONIE   Actually, no. I'll have a tea as well.

PRESTON   Ordinary or Early Grey?

LEONIE   Ordinary.

            (PRESTON *starts to leave.*)

LEONIE   No. Early Grey. Earl Grey.

PRESTON   Gotcha. Early Grey. With milk?

LEONIE   Yes, please.

            (Again, PRESTON *starts to leave.*)

LEONIE   Oh, no! You've only got full fat milk, haven't you?

PRESTON   For real!

LEONIE   I'll just have water.

PRESTON   Ice?

LEONIE   Yeah.

            (PRESTON *starts to leave again.*)

LEONIE   And a bit of lemon, if you've got it.

PRESTON   We ain't got no lemon.

LEONIE   Oh. Well, that's fine.

            (PRESTON *moves to go again.*)

LEONIE   Actually, can I have an orange juice instead.

PRESTON   You can have anything you want, Leonie . . . and a
            little bit more.

LEONIE   (*not picking up on* PRESTON's *flirting*) Great.

PRESTON   One Early Grey. One orange juice, yeah?

PHIL   (*patiently*) I think that's about the size of it.

            (PRESTON *is about to leave.*)

LEONIE   (*to* PRESTON) And have you got any croissants?

PRESTON   Yeah, we have, but they've been around all
              morning so they're probably a bit skanky.

PHIL   I'm sure they're not.

LEONIE   Oh, I keep forgetting what time it is. No. I'll wait
              'til lunch.

PRESTON   D'you want me to bring you the menu, yeah?

LEONIE   That's an idea.

PHIL   He's full of ideas, aren't you?

              (PRESTON *turns to go.*)

LEONIE   Actually, I'll wait 'til the boys get here and see
              what they want.

PRESTON   Awesome!

PHIL   Truly!

JULIAN   Is there a script I can look at? (*To himself.*) Oh, I'm
              not 'up' . . .

              (*No one can hear him. He waves at* PHIL.)

PHIL   Sorry, matey. You weren't 'up'.

JULIAN   I was just wondering if there was a script I can
              look at.

              (PHIL *turns to look at* LEONIE.)

LEONIE   The boys are bringing it . . . (*To* PHIL.) Can he hear
              me?

PHIL   You need to press your talkback button.

LEONIE   Where's my head?

              (LEONIE *looks for the talkback button. She can't
              see it.*)

PHIL   By your bum . . .

               (*She can't see it.*)

PHIL   By the magazines.

               (*She can't see it.*)

LEONIE   Err . . .

               (PHIL *wheels back and presses it for her.* LEONIE *sees it and takes over.*)

LEONIE   Oh! Thanks! (*To* JULIAN.) The boys are bringing the script.

JULIAN   Okay. I'll just get on with my Sudoku.

PHIL   Help yourself to a pencil, matey.

JULIAN   Ah! The legendary pencils!

PHIL   You know me!

               (JULIAN *ceremoniously takes a pencil from a pot of pencils and begins a Sudoku.*)

PHIL   Of course, they say, 'In London, you're never more than six feet away from a Sudoku.'

JULIAN   I thought that was rats.

PHIL   Rats *and* Sudokus.

JULIAN   What about rats doing Sudokus?

PHIL   That's seven feet.

               (PHIL *shuts off his side of the talkback.*)

LEONIE   (*concerned about the time*) I don't know where they are.

               (JULIAN *blows out his lips to help warm-up his voice.*)

LEONIE   What's that?

PHIL   Julian. Warming up. I'll fade him.

              (*The door bursts open as* DINO *and* WES *enter,
              waving an award.* DINO *also clutches a handful of
              scripts.*)

DINO/WES   (*like football fans*) "Championes-championes, we
              are the champions! Championes-championes . . ."

LEONIE   Yes. Well done.

WES   Thank you very much!

DINO   Thank you!

LEONIE   What was it for?

DINO   Best . . . (*To* WES.) What was it?

WES   (*reading*) "Best Radio Commercial – funny –
              outside London – for 'New Tesco', Knutsford."

PHIL   Congratulations!

WES   Thanks, pal!

LEONIE   Oh, this is Phil. Phil, Wes.

WES   And this is Dino – my right hand man. The Galton
              to my Simpson. The Merchant to my Gervais. The
              pain in my arse!

DINO   Steady! (*To* PHIL.) I think we've met before,
              actually.

PHIL   Several times. The first thing we did was
              "Campbell's Meatballs."

DINO   Yeah, that's right . . .

WES   (*disparagingly*) You wrote that?

DINO   I was very young.

WES   That shite old jingle!

DINO	Yeah.
WES	Number nine in 'The One Hundred Most Irritating Ads Ever' on Channel 4?
DINO	Yes!
WES	(*sings to the verse of 'The Can-Can'*) 'Jo loves Campbell's meatballs . . .'
DINO	'And they say 'we love you'!'
PHIL	(*to* DINO) That was it!
WES	Shite! Utter shite!
DINO	(*a nod to* PHIL) It was very well produced!
PHIL	Must have been '96?
WES	(*putting an arm round* DINO) Before I saved him from the scrapheap and made him a multi-award-winning writer!
JULIAN	(*making a Sudoku error*) Bollocks!
PHIL	Sorry, I forgot I hadn't faded him down.
	(PHIL *fades him down.*)
WES	(*shocked*) Who's that?
DINO	Julian Mann.
WES	What happened to Matt Lucas?
LEONIE	He pulled out late last night.
WES	What? Why?
LEONIE	Some film he's doing with Ben Stiller. His agent said they'd changed the dates or something.
WES	Bloody agents!
PHIL	Julian's very good.

WES   But he's not Matt Lucas!

DINO   Sorry. I meant to tell you last night but I got
               dragged away by . . .

JULIAN   (*now unheard by them*) Peggy Babcock. Peggy
               Babcock. Peggy Babcock.

DINO   Anyway, this guy's very versatile.

PHIL   Probably more versatile than Matt Lucas, actually.

WES   (*sarcastic*) Yeah, right.

PHIL   Probably.

LEONIE   Was it written specially for Matt Lucas?

DINO   No. Wes just wanted to meet Matt Lucas, didn't
               you?

WES   Yeah.

PHIL   Right.

DINO   (*to* WES) I'm sure this guy's very good.

WES   Yeah, but my little girl isn't going to be very
               happy when I tell her I didn't work with 'the only
               gay in the village', I worked with Julian . . . (*To*
               PHIL.) What?

PHIL   Mann.

WES   Mann. Is she?

DINO   He can't hear us, can he?

PHIL   No.

JULIAN   Mrs Puggy-Wuggy had a square-cut punt. Not a
               punt cut square but a square-cut punt . . .

LEONIE   We really should get on – we've only got the
               hour.

PHIL   Less than that now.

WES   And where's the woman? What'shername?

LEONIE   Late.

PHIL   Ten minutes late.

JULIAN   It was round at the stern but blunt at the front;
            Mrs Puggy-Wuggy had a square-cut putt . . .

            (PHIL *picks up the phone on his desk.*)

LEONIE   (*via talkback*) Hi, Julian!

JULIAN   Hi! (*Looking up.*) Oh, more guests at the party!

LEONIE   (*to* WES *and* DINO) D'you want him to come
            through and I'll introduce him?

WES   We'll just wave.

LEONIE   (*via talkback*) This is Wes and Dino, the
            creatives.

            (*They wave.*)

JULIAN   I'll come through.

WES   He's coming through.

PHIL   (*into phone*) Hi, Kirsty! Have you had any sort of
            message from . . . ?

LEONIE   Amanda Birmingham.

PHIL   (*slightly reeling*) Amanda?

LEONIE   Birmingham.

PHIL   Amanda Birmingham to say she's running late?

            (PRESTON *enters with drinks on a tray.*)

PRESTON   Amanda's running late. Should be here in five
            minutes, innit?

PHIL   When did that message come through?

PRESTON   About five minutes ago.

PHIL   So, are we talking five minutes from now or five
                minutes from then?

PRESTON   From then.

PHIL   Right. Thanks. (*To phone.*) Thanks. (*To* LEONIE.)
                She'll be here any minute – apparently.

                (PHIL *puts the phone down.*)

PRESTON   One orange juice . . .

LEONIE   Thanks Preston.

PRESTON   Freshly squeezed.

                (JULIAN *enters.*)

JULIAN   (*extending his hand*) Julian Mann.

WES   We're so glad you're doing this!

DINO   Yeah. Big fan!

WES   Me too!

JULIAN   Really?

WES   Oh, yeah!

JULIAN   Well, thank you.

DINO   Yeah. Your demo's just . . . great!

LEONIE   I played it to him on the website.

                (PRESTON *gives* JULIAN *his tea.*)

JULIAN   We did that here, didn't we, Phil?

PHIL   Ironically. Many moons ago!

DINO   Who'd have thought you could say, 'Can't find
            the right man? Call *Julian* Mann!' in so many
            different ways?!

JULIAN   Fifty-one.

DINO   Wow! Is it Fifty-one?

JULIAN   Ten actual impressions; ten cartoon voices;
            twenty English accents; eleven World accents . . .
            fifty-one.

PHIL   He's 'The man of a Thousand Voices'!

JULIAN   Well, fifty-one!

WES   Can you do Matt Lucas?

JULIAN   Who's he?

WES   Who's he? *Little Britain*.

JULIAN   Oh, I've never seen that.

WES   How can you never have seen *Little Britain*?

JULIAN   I don't watch much TV – can't bear all the
            wretched ads!

WES   It's on BBC.

PHIL   Actually, it's also on 'Dave' where they do have
            wretched ads . . .

JULIAN   I only have terrestrial.

DINO   Really?

WES   My kids would go mad without Nickleodeon. *I'd*
            go mad without Nickleodeon.

PRESTON   Did you two dreds want anything to drink, yeah?

DINO   Can I have a tea? No sugar.

PRESTON   For real, dred.

Wes	And I'll have . . . actually, I'll have a beer.
Dino	Already?
Wes	Yes.
Preston	We've got Stella. Is that alright?
Wes	(*to* Dino) Is that alright?
Dino	Do what you like, mate.
Wes	Stella is fine.
	(Preston *leaves.*)
Wes	(*puzzled*) What did he call us?
Dino	'Dreds'.
Wes	Right.
Leonie	Random!
Phil	So, the script . . . ?
Leonie	Oh, yeah.
Wes	Oh, yeah.
	(Wes *hands a script to* Julian *and to everyone else.*)
Wes	This probably won't take long; we'll be in the pub by half past!
Dino	Figuratively speaking.
Wes	Honestly speaking.
Julian	(*looking at the script*) Am I doing both male parts?
Dino	Is that okay?
Julian	Sure. And the end-line?
Dino	Yeah.

PHIL   You're getting your money's worth!

JULIAN   I'll have to charge triple time!

            (*The creatives all look at him, horrified.*)

JULIAN   Not really! And the FVO?

WES   The FVO?

JULIAN   I do 'do' women – as you'll know from the
            website.

WES   Yes. But no.

LEONIE   (*sotto*) 'Yes but no but.' Ha!

JULIAN   What?

LEONIE   Nothing.

WES   We've got someone coming in to do the FVO.

JULIAN   Okay.

LEONIE   We hope!

JULIAN   I did once play one of the three witches from 'The
            Scottish Play' in some dreadful ad with Dawn
            French and, err . . .

PHIL   Jane Horrocks . . .

JULIAN   Jane Horrocks! Was that here?

PHIL   Yeah. 1998.

LEONIE   This guy's memory!

JULIAN   I never heard that ad. And I used to listen to them
            all back then.

PHIL   It never went out. We recorded a new ad with
            Alexei Sayle later that day.

JULIAN   Oh, the power of fame, eh?

WES   I love Alexei Sayle! We should've got him in.
            (*imitating*) 'Hello, Tosh! Got a Toshiba?' 'Hello,
            Tosh! Got a Toshiba?'– Genius! (WES *stands and
            paces, slowly kicking a leg out on each 'Hey!'*)
            'Doctor Marten's Boots. Hey! Doctor Marten's
            Boots! Hey! Doctor Marten's, Doctor Marten's,
            Doctor Marten's Boots! Hey!' Remember that?

LEONIE   No.

WES   *The Young Ones*.

LEONIE   I'm too young.

WES   Jesus!

LEONIE   Wes!

WES   What?

DINO   (*coughs*) Lord's name!

WES   Oh! Sorry!

LEONIE   (*to* DINO) Thank you.

DINO   A-ny-way . . .

LEONIE   Yes.

DINO   We're not sure what we want exactly.

WES   (*sotto*) Well, We *were* sure.

DINO   Just . . . see how it comes out.

LEONIE   Yeah, anything you can give us, really.

JULIAN   Okay. Is there anything we can do without our
            FVO?

DINO   Not really, no.

JULIAN   I'll go through anyway.

PHIL   Right.

JULIAN   Back to my Sudoku . . .

DINO	Oh, I'm addicted!
JULIAN	Really?
DINO	Yeah. My girlfriend calls them 'Sod-you-okays'.
WES	Here we go . . .
DINO	You know, the newspaper goes up and it's like, 'Sod you, okay!'
JULIAN	Nice!
WES	You and your fuckin' perfect little home life! 'I'm just going to do a Sudoku, darling.' 'A 'Sod-you-okay?' Well, I'll just go and put my diaphragm in so I'm ready for you when you're finished.' Mr Bleedin' Stepford!

(*The door opens and* AMANDA BIRMINGHAM *enters, late – a flurry of coats and skirts and bags and hair. She walks past* JULIAN, *who is up against the door jamb, without seeing him.*)

AMANDA	I am so sorry! (*Frantic.*) Did you get my message?
PHIL	We did.
AMANDA	Oh, good!
PHIL	Finally.
AMANDA	I'm so sorry!
LEONIE	Don't worry. Really!
AMANDA	I had a costume fitting for a Dickens thing I'm doing and we just couldn't find the right shoes for her – my character. I find it all depends on the shoes. Old-fashioned, I know but if I don't feel rooted I can't . . . Oh, you don't want to know. Anyway, sorry! (*To* PHIL.) Sorry!
LEONIE	It's really so fine.

WES   (*offering his hand*) I'm Wes, the writer – and this
              is Dino.

DINO   (*ditto*) The *other* writer.

AMANDA   Hi! Hi!

LEONIE   (*waving*) And I'm Leonie, from MBSTWD and D –
              producer.

AMANDA   Hi! 'Leonie' – what a pretty name!

LEONIE   Oh, thanks!

AMANDA   And I'm loving those boots!

LEONIE   Stella McCartney.

AMANDA   I thought so. How much were they?

LEONIE   I don't know; I was given them.

AMANDA   By 'your man'?

LEONIE   By Stella McCartney.

DINO   Shall we start?

PHIL   Or shall we talk about shoes a bit longer?

AMANDA   Sorry.

PHIL   I'm Phil.

LEONIE   Sorry, I assumed you two had met.

AMANDA   No. Hi, Phil!

PHIL   Actually, we *did* do one last week for 'Danone'.

AMANDA   Sorry! Of course we did! Yes. (*Sings.*) 'Umm,
              Danone!'

LEONIE   And this is Julian Mann our other voice.

JULIAN   (*to* LEONIE) '. . . over artist.'

LEONIE   'Voice-over artist', sorry. Terrible habit.

PHIL	Terrible.
AMANDA	(*seeing* JULIAN) Hi. Hi. Julian.
JULIAN	Hello, Amanda. Nice to see you.
AMANDA	You too. Yes.
JULIAN	Yes.
AMANDA	Good.
PHIL	(*to* WES *and* DINO) Are your phones off?
DINO	Yes.
JULIAN	Weird. I was only thinking about you the other day too.
PHIL	Tel-e-pathy!!
AMANDA	Yes.
PHIL	'There are more things in heaven and earth, Horatio, than . . . something'.
LEONIE	What?
DINO	Othello.
PHIL	Hamlet.
DINO	Yes.
LEONIE	Oh! I did PPE.
WES	PPE? What is that?
JULIAN	PE for someone with a stutter.
PHIL	Politics, philosophy and . . .
AMANDA	Shall we go through? I've probably kept you all waiting long enough.
JULIAN	After you.

WES	(*leaping up*) Ooh, Amanda! There's a script for you.
AMANDA	Might need that, eh?
	(*They leave for the booth.*)
LEONIE	(*looking at her watch*) We're a bit tight for time now.
PHIL	Julian's always very quick.
WES	She was gorgeous!
DINO	Much prettier in the flesh!
	(JULIAN *and* AMANDA *arrive in the booth, silently.*)
WES	Yeah, she always looks so dowdy in *Eastenders* but she's really fwuft! Really fwuft!
DINO	I thought you were quiet.
WES	She can't hear me, can she?
PHIL	No.
WES	Pity!
DINO	Jesus!
LEONIE	Oi!
DINO	Sorry!
WES	Is she married?
LEONIE	I don't know.
DINO	But *you* are.
WES	Just.
LEONIE	You're dreadful!
WES	So I'm always told.
JULIAN	I didn't know you did these.

AMANDA	I've only just started – doing these.
LEONIE	(*to* WES) You know, according to Christian doctrine, even looking at another woman in a lustful way constitutes infidelity.
WES	Then God help me!
LEONIE	Maybe he would.
DINO	He'd have his work cut out.
WES	Alright, Goldenballs!
JULIAN	(*to* AMANDA) So, who're you with?
AMANDA	What?
JULIAN	Who's your agent?
AMANDA	Oh, for these? 'Chatterbox.'
JULIAN	Don't know them.
AMANDA	They've got some people. I mean, they've got some good people. Of course, they've got 'people'.
JULIAN	Of course they have.
AMANDA	Jack Davenport is one of their . . . ermm . . .
JULIAN	'People?'
AMANDA	Yes. And Michael Gambon.
JULIAN	Ah. 'Gambon!'
AMANDA	Yeah, he's a Chatterbox . . . err . . . person.
WES	I think he fancies her too, old Julian!
PHIL	Shall we do one?

DINO	He did blush like a . . . great big blushing thing when he saw her.
LEONIE	(*to* PHIL) Yes.
WES	I just go quiet in front of beautiful women like that.
DINO	We should introduce you to a few more.
WES	I wish you bleedin' would!
LEONIE	Going live! (*She presses the button.*) Hi, guys! Shall we have a little read on tape and get some timings?
JULIAN	Sure.
AMANDA	Can I just have a quick glance at it?
LEONIE	Sure!
AMANDA	I did ask my agent to send it through last night but she said you were having technical problems.
	(LEONIE *takes her finger off the button.*)
WES	(*sotto*) Yeah. Like we hadn't fucking written it!
DINO	That's not strictly true.
LEONIE	Actually, I haven't read the final version yet.
	(*A silence as* LEONIE, PHIL, AMANDA *and* JULIAN *all read it.* DINO *and* WES *reach for the sweet jar and the fruit bowl.*)
WES	Where's the client? Whatshername?
LEONIE	Jenny? She couldn't make it. 'Meetings'. We've got to play it down the line to her later.
DINO	I hate that!
WES	(*to* PHIL) Hey, Pal! Didn't I ask for a Stella about half a bleedin' hour ago?

(PHIL *lifts his phone and presses a number.*)

PHIL   Any sign of that Stella? Yes. And a tea. And . . .
              Hang on . . . (*He presses his button to the studio.*)
              Amanda? Sorry. Amanda? Did you want a drink?

AMANDA   I'm fine. We won't be long, will we?

WES   Hope not!

PHIL   (*releasing his talkback*) Just the Stella and a tea.

              (AMANDA *waves madly.*)

PHIL   (*via talkback*) Sorry?

AMANDA   Actually, can I have an orange juice?

PHIL   (*release talkback, then into the phone*) And an
              orange juice.

JULIAN   Bad for the voice.

AMANDA   What?

JULIAN   Orange juice. It's acidic. Not great
                              before you work.

AMANDA   I'll bear that in mind.

DINO   Aren't 'Twirls' under-rated?

JULIAN   How are you then?

AMANDA   Oh! Fine. You?

JULIAN   Yes. Good. Really good.

AMANDA   That's good.

DINO   The Aston Villa of chocolates.

AMANDA   I should really read this.

JULIAN   Of course. Of course.

WES   Or the Harry Redknapp.

AMANDA	I like the short hair, by the way.
PHIL	Harry is underrated.
JULIAN	It's been short ever since . . .
LEONIE	(*to* DINO *and* WES) It's nice – I think the cuts work well.
WES	We haven't cut anything.
DINO	We put some extra bits in.
LEONIE	Oh. Well, it reads well.
DINO	Like the new end-line?
LEONIE	Ve-ery nice!
DINO	Just came to me this morning in the shower.
WES	As long as that's all that came this morning in the shower! I thank you!
AMANDA	This is dreadful!
JULIAN	What?
AMANDA	The script.
	(LEONIE *presses the button.*)
LEONIE	Shall we have a read?
AMANDA	It's really funny!
DINO	Cheers.
WES	Thanks.
AMANDA	Have you got any hints on how you want it?
LEONIE	Not really.
WES	No.
DINO	No.

AMANDA   Okay.

WES   They're just a couple who've been together a few years, out in the car – they're a bit late and a bit lost, you know?

JULIAN   Okay.

AMANDA   Right.

DINO   I suppose we don't want it to sound too voice-over-y though, d'you know what I mean?

LEONIE   Yeah, it should sound very . . . natural.

WES   But tense.

LEONIE   Naturally tense.

DINO   (*to* WES *and* LEONIE) That's in the writing – the tension. They don't need to act the tension.

WES   No . . . But it should be there.

DINO   Oh, yeah! It should definitely be there.

LEONIE   (*to* JULIAN *and* AMANDA) Just do it how you want, really.

JULIAN   No accents?

WES   Just as your very good selves.

PHIL   Okay. This is "VM Vogel Sat Nav . . ."

AMANDA   Where are they going, by the way?

WES   Just . . . out. It doesn't really matter, does it?

AMANDA   Okay.

JULIAN   It's not Chekhov . . .

AMANDA   No but . . . Well, anyway.

PHIL   Okay. This is VM Vogel Sat Nav – No Argument . . ."

JULIAN   Sorry, do you want me to do the end-line now as
            well or will we do that separately?

PHIL   We'll do it separately but just read it now for me,
            matey, so that we get a timing.

JULIAN   Okay, matey.

AMANDA   And it's twenty seconds?

WES   Thirty seconds.

AMANDA   My agent said it was twenty seconds.

WES   It was. But we got another ten.

LEONIE   Bought another ten.

DINO   Yeah, from a geezer outside a pub in Soho!

WES   But they weren't new.

LEONIE   What?

DINO   They were 'seconds'!

DINO/WES   I thank you!

PHIL   It's thirty seconds, Amanda.

AMANDA   Okay.

PHIL   Okay, this is . . .

AMANDA   (*to* JULIAN) Do we get any more for that?

            (JULIAN *shakes his head.*)

PHIL   . . . VM Vogel Sat Nav – 'No Argument'. Take one.

            (*The recording commences.*)

AMANDA   We've gone too far!

JULIAN   We have *not* gone too far!

AMANDA   We have! Look! That was Bourton Road and
            Bourton Road is after Blockley Road not before it!

JULIAN	You've got the map upside down!
AMANDA	It's called orienteering!
JULIAN	It's the next left.
AMANDA	So, you know more than the map?
JULIAN	Perhaps there's a mistake on it.
AMANDA	Yeah, they probably deliberately put mistakes on maps to make driving more exciting!

(JULIAN *grunts.*)

AMANDA	Let's ask this man . . .
JULIAN	It's the next left!
AMANDA	Excuse me, which way is Blockley Road?
JULIAN	(*rural accent*) Oh, you've gone way past it, love. It's . . .
AMANDA	(*very self-satisfied*) That's all I wanted to know . . .
JULIAN	(*voice-over voice*) The new VM Vogel has Sat Nav fitted as standard. It gets you there – no argument!
WES	(*clapping*) Brilliant! Brilliant!
PHIL	Do you want them to hear you?
WES	(*exasperated*) Yes!

(PHIL *presses the talkback button.*)

WES	That was great!
LEONIE	It's really funny!
AMANDA	I wasn't sure how to do her but was that okay?
WES	It was superb, Amanda!
LEONIE	Really good!

AMANDA	Are you sure?
WES	Abso-bloody-lutely!
JULIAN	I don't know why I did 'the man' rural but it just seemed to fit.
WES	Yeah. (*To* PHIL.) How was that for time, pal?
PHIL	Twenty eight seconds. So that leaves us two seconds for effects. Perfect!
WES	(*punching the air*) In one!
LEONIE	(*to* JULIAN *and* AMANDA) Just relax in there – we'll have a bit of a pow-wow.
	(PHIL *turns off the talkback.*)
LEONIE	Happy?
WES	Yep!
LEONIE	Dino?
DINO	I didn't like it.
WES	What?!
LEONIE	The script or the performances?
DINO	No, the script's fine.
LEONIE	I think the script's good.
PHIL	Very good.
WES	I thought it was raw – they really got that sense of a couple who are starting to fuckin' hate each other.
LEONIE	The end-line was nice too.
PHIL	Julian *is* Mr End-line.
WES	And she was great! Gorgeous and great!

(AMANDA *is playing with the large jar of pencils during the 'silence'.*)

AMANDA   (*to* JULIAN) What a lot of pencils.

DINO   I don't know . . .

JULIAN   Watch yourself! Phil likes to keep
                    them really sharp.

AMANDA   Thanks. I'm always worried I might be
                    penciled to death.

DINO   (*to* PHIL *and* LEONIE) We've got an hour, yeah?

PHIL   Yeah. With a possible . . .

WES   I really don't think you'll get it better than that.

LEONIE   Why don't we have a listeny-back and then we
            can decide?

WES   You'll love it when you hear it.

AMANDA   I always wonder what they're saying.

JULIAN   Yeah.

DINO   Yeah.

AMANDA   I always think it's me.

DINO   (*to* WES *and* LEONIE) I'm just not sure about her.

JULIAN   I'm sure it's not.

WES   What?!

JULIAN   They seemed happy.

AMANDA   I always worry I'm too . . . 'stagey'.

LEONIE   She is a bit 'stagey'.

AMANDA   Why are they shaking their heads?

JULIAN   They're probably ordering
                sandwiches or something.

                (LEONIE *presses the talkback.*)

LEONIE   Soz, guys. We're just going to have a listeny-
                back. Do you want to hear it?

JULIAN   No, that's fine.

AMANDA   Yes, please!

PHIL   Playing back.

                (*We hear the whole advert back as they sit and
                listen.* WES *paces around, laughing far too much
                at anything remotely intended to be funny.*)

AMANDA   *WE'VE GONE TOO FAR!*

JULIAN   *WE HAVE NOT GONE TOO FAR!*

AMANDA   *WE HAVE! LOOK! THAT WAS BOURTON ROAD AND
                BOURTON ROAD IS AFTER BLOCKLEY ROAD NOT BEFORE
                IT!*

JULIAN   *YOU'VE GOT THE MAP UPSIDE DOWN!*

AMANDA   *IT'S CALLED ORIENTEERING!*

JULIAN   *IT'S THE NEXT LEFT.*

AMANDA   *SO, YOU KNOW MORE THAN THE MAP?*

JULIAN   *PERHAPS THERE'S A MISTAKE ON IT.*

AMANDA   *YEAH, THEY PROBABLY DELIBERATELY PUT MISTAKES ON
                MAPS TO MAKE DRIVING MORE EXCITING!*

                (JULIAN *GRUNTS.*)

AMANDA   *LET'S ASK THIS MAN . . .*

JULIAN   *IT'S THE NEXT LEFT!*

AMANDA   *EXCUSE ME, WHICH WAY IS BLOCKLEY ROAD?*

JULIAN   (*RURAL ACCENT*) O*H, YOU'VE GONE WAY PAST IT, LOVE.*
            I*T'S* . . .

AMANDA   (*VERY SELF-SATISFIED*) T*HAT'S ALL* I *WANTED TO KNOW* . . .

JULIAN   (*VOICE-OVER VOICE*) T*HE NEW* VM V*OGEL HAS* S*AT* N*AV*
            FITTED AS STANDARD. IT GETS YOU THERE — *NO*
            ARGUMENT!

            (*As it ends,* PHIL *hits a button and sits back.*)

WES   Good, yeah?

DINO   Better than I thought.

PHIL   Do you want to hear it with the effects?

WES   I think we can imagine the effects, pal.

PHIL   It won't take a second.

WES   You're fine.

AMANDA   (*to* JULIAN) God, it's like facing a
                                firing squad.

            (WES *presses the talkback.*)

WES   I think we've got it there.

AMANDA   Really?

WES   How can you improve on perfection?

JULIAN   As long as you're happy.

            (JULIAN *bends to pick up his things.*)

WES   (*to* JULIAN) Off down the pub?

JULIAN   Well, maybe a quick trip to Waterstones.

WES   Yeah, yeah! Mine's a Stella.

            (LEONIE *takes her hand off the talkback.*)

AMANDA   Still an avid reader, then?

JULIAN   Yeah. I've got a whole room full of
                                books now. Wall to wall.

                                (AMANDA *and* JULIAN *stand and start to gather
                                their things, put coats on, etc.*)

PHIL   That was painless.

AMANDA   I think it's called a library.

DINO   Wes?

JULIAN   Yeah.

WES   What?!

JULIAN   Although I haven't got any old
                                people in there keeping warm for free.

AMANDA   As far as you know.

JULIAN   As far as I know.

DINO   Shall we just try something else?

WES   Job done, mate.

DINO   (*to* LEONIE) But we've booked them for an hour,
            right?

LEONIE   With a possible half-hour over-run. Amanda's got
            to be away by 1.30.

WES   Pity! I was going to ask her for a drink.

JULIAN   (*to* AMANDA) Drink?

LEONIE   Wes!

WES   Only a quick one!

AMANDA   I have to go, really.

DINO   I just think, you know, there might be something
            better.

WES	I used to think that but there never is.
PHIL	It's always worth a try!
JULIAN	Of course. Pity but . . .
WES	(*to* PHIL) You think it's not good?
PHIL	No. I think it's very good. Very good. But . . .
JULIAN	I understand.
PHIL	. . . Julian's very versatile.
DINO	And I just think she's not there yet.
WES	Not there? So, where is she? I can see her! There she is!
AMANDA	You understand?
DINO	I mean, she's not quite 'up' enough.
LEONIE	Shall I stop them?
JULIAN	(*to* AMANDA) Nice coat, by the way.
AMANDA	Thanks.
JULIAN	Didn't I buy you one like that once?
LEONIE	Well?
AMANDA	Very similar.
DINO	Stop them.
WES	Jesus!
LEONIE	Wes!
	(PHIL *presses the talkback.*)
PHIL	(*interrupts – à la Bogart*) Not so fast, Miss Birmingham!
AMANDA	Oh?

LEONIE	Soz, guys. Can we just do one more?
JULIAN	Yes, of course!
AMANDA	I thought we'd got off lightly!
JULIAN	It's why we're here, after all.
	(*They begin to settle down again.*)
LEONIE	We just want to try errr . . . (*She takes her finger off the talkback.*) What do we want to try?
WES	Dino?
DINO	What?
WES	What *do* we want to try?
DINO	I don't know. Can we just try one with . . .
LEONIE	They can't hear you.
	(*She presses the talkback.*)
DINO	Can we just try one that's a bit more . . . 'up'?
AMANDA	Up?
DINO	Yeah, you know.
AMANDA	Sorry. Louder?
PHIL	No, no. Volume's fine. (*To* DINO.) Isn't it?
DINO	Yeah. No, I mean, more, 'into the argument'.
JULIAN	On both sides?
DINO	More hers, really. He's fine. He's nicely cowed.
JULIAN	Thanks. 'Cowed' has always been my speciality!
WES	I know the feeling!
DINO	I just think she can be more . . . 'up'.
AMANDA	Okay.

(PRESTON *appears at the portal window.* PHIL
*gestures him in. He is carrying a round, plastic
tray with the three drinks on.*)

WES   Ah! The slowest barman in the world returns!

PRESTON   Sorry, about that, dred. One Stella . . .

            (*He hands* WES *his Stella.*)

WES   You nearly missed us, 'dred'. (*He sips it straight
            away.*)

PRESTON   One tea . . .

            (*He hands* DINO *his tea.*)

WES   Have you not got a cold one?

PRESTON   That's from out the fridge, mate.

WES   It's not very cold, 'mate'.

AMANDA   (*to* JULIAN) How's the Sudoku?

PRESTON   You want me to get you some ice?

WES   Ice in Stella?

JULIAN   I went wrong.

WES   What planet do you come from?

            (PRESTON *leaves with the orange juice.*)

DINO   Wes, he's just a kid.

WES   Well! Ice? In Stella?

JULIAN   (*to* AMANDA) And once you've gone
                         wrong, there's no way back with
                         these fellas.

LEONIE   (*to* WES) Is it warm?

WES   It's not cold.

JULIAN   (*to* AMANDA) 'Cos you can't ever find
                out where you've gone wrong.

WES   It's vaguely chilled.

JULIAN   You just know it's not going to work
                out, don't you?

AMANDA   I've never done one.

                (PRESTON *enters the booth, with the orange juice.*)

PRESTON   One orange juice . . .

AMANDA   Thanks.

PRESTON   Is it cold enough?

AMANDA   I'm sure it's just right.

WES   There's nothing worse than a warm beer!

PHIL   Crucifixion?

WES   Close.

                (PRESTON *goes.* AMANDA *sips her orange juice.*)

JULIAN   Bad for the voice . . .

AMANDA   Thanks, 'Dad'.

PHIL   All set?

                (AMANDA *and* JULIAN *nod.* LEONIE *presses the
                talkback.*)

LEONIE   So more 'up', guys, yeah?

                (*She lets go of the talkback.* AMANDA *and* JULIAN
                nod.)

DINO   *She's* got to be more up.

WES   She knows.

PHIL   VM – No Argument. Take Two . . .

(The recording begins again. Amanda *is more aggressive.)*

AMANDA   We've gone too far!

JULIAN   We have *not* gone too far!

AMANDA   We have! Look! That was Bourton Road and Burton Road is . . . Sorry! I said 'Burton',didn't I? It's 'Bourton,' isn't it? *(To* JULIAN.*)* Isn't it?

JULIAN   Yeah. Bourton. I'd say Bourton. *(To the creatives.)* Is it Bourton?

DINO   I think she's too 'up' now.

JULIAN   Not listening.

LEONIE   Yeah, it's throwing her.

PHIL   *(via talkback)* A bit less 'up', Amanda.

AMANDA   Okay.

PHIL   And . . . three!

            (The recording begins again.)

AMANDA   We've gone too far!

JULIAN   We have *not* gone too far!

AMANDA   We have! Look!

DINO   *(to the team)* It's gone down.

AMANDA   That was Bourton Road and Bourton Road is after Blockley Road not before it!

DINO   *(via talkback)* Sorry. It's gone 'down' again. Keep it 'up'.

WES   Yeah. Maybe think of that couple in *Pulp Fiction* – it's them, really . . . That's what the scene's based on, isn't it?

DINO   Yeah, that's what it's based on. *Pulp Fiction*,
            yeah.

JULIAN   Love Tarantino!

WES   The couple in the car – just after they've shot the
            guy's brains out. That's what it's based on.

DINO   That's what it's based on.

LEONIE   (*to* PHIL) Do you think that's clear?

PHIL   Oh, it's VERY clear!

AMANDA   So, is it his wife or are they just 'partners'?

WES   They're just 'a couple' – it doesn't matter, does it?

LEONIE   Have they got children?

DINO   What?

LEONIE   Have they got children? Maybe we should put
            some children in the back.

WES   (*enthusiastic*) Just like that! Because we can! You
            want children? Bang! Children! I love it! The
            power of advertising! We are Gods?

DINO   You want them to have children?

WES   (*suddenly off the idea*) Nah! We'll have to give
            them lines; we haven't got time.

PHIL   I could just put some children in, in the
            background, afterwards.

WES   Children are never 'in the background' when
            you're in a car – lost!

PHIL   Okay.

WES   Mine bloody aren't!

PHIL   So, they haven't got children?

LEONIE	No.
WES	Lucky things!
DINO	No children.
WES	Hey! Maybe that's why there's the extra tension! They want them but can't have them!
LEONIE	I like it!
PHIL	Nice!
WES	(*to* DINO) Eh?
DINO	(*sadly*) Yeah. Nice. I'm clearly a better writer than I thought.
WES	You're a fuckin' award-winner! Wa-hey!
	(WES *picks up the advertising trophy from the night before and waves it in* DINO'S *face.*)
DINO	Stop it!
LEONIE	Boys, boys!
PHIL	Did you get all that?
AMANDA	Loud and clear!
PHIL	So, this is take . . . what is it?
LEONIE	Three.
PHIL	Four.
LEONIE	Four.
	(*The recording begins again.*)
AMANDA	We've gone too far!
JULIAN	We have *not* gone too far!
AMANDA	We have! Look! That was Bourton Road and Bourley Road is . . . Oh!

LEONIE   Don't worry!

AMANDA   Sorry, it's all those 'B's'! It is quite a mouthful,
                actually – 'That was Bourton Road and Bourton
                Road is after Blockley Road not before it.' Sorry.

JULIAN   (*teasing*) If you hadn't had that
                               orange juice.

AMANDA   Yeah, that would have made all the
                               difference.

JULIAN   It's the acid – eating away at your
                               larynx.

AMANDA   Thanks, Jules.

JULIAN   (*making eating noises*) Nyum-nyum-
                               nyum-nyum!

AMANDA   Shut up!

JULIAN   (*waggling his fingers at her*) Nyum-
                               nyum-nyum-nyum! Mr Eaty Man!

AMANDA   Stop it!

PHIL   Happy to go again?

JULIAN   Sorry! Getting carried away in here.

WES   Perfectly understandable!

AMANDA   Hang on. (*She has a swig of water.*)

LEONIE   (*to* DINO) Where are Bourton Road and Blockley
                Road?

DINO   They're just places in the Cotswolds.

WES   I thought you'd made them up.

DINO   No.

LEONIE	Can we change them?
AMANDA	(*to* JULIAN) Och, they're talking again!
DINO	(*to* LEONIE) Why do you want to change them?
LEONIE	Well, it is a mouthful.
JULIAN	(*to* AMANDA) How are you, then? Really?
WES	Why did you choose those names?
AMANDA	Well, good. Yeah. In general. You?
DINO	I was driving round there at the weekend with Suzi.
JULIAN	Yeah. In general.
DINO	We wanted to take our minds off . . .
JULIAN	Well, pretty shit actually.
DINO	Oh, I just thought they sounded like the sort of places where you might get lost.
WES	But no one's heard of these places!
DINO	Well, that's why you get lost. Why *they're* lost!
WES	I think we should change them.
DINO	What, just 'cos 'your girlfriend' can't pronounce them?
LEONIE	It'll save us time in the long run.
AMANDA	I'm sure they hate me.
JULIAN	I'm sure they don't; everyone always loves you.

WES	I just think there's something funnier.
JULIAN	(*not bitter*) They always did. They always will. I know, I . . .

(LEONIE *reaches for the talkback button and presses it.*)

LEONIE	Sorry, guys! We're just thinking of changing the names of the roads.
AMANDA	Not because I stumbled?
LEONIE	No!
WES	No!
PHIL	No!
AMANDA	I'm just a bit thrown by the whole . . .
LEONIE	(*interrupting*) We're wondering if there's something funnier, guys. We'll just have a bit of a pow-wow.
JULIAN	Okay.

(LEONIE *takes her finger off the talkback.*)

PHIL	'K's are always funny.
WES	What?
PHIL	'K's' are funny. That's what Rik Mayall used to say.
AMANDA	(*to* JULIAN) I hate the way she calls us 'guys'.
WES	You worked with Rik Mayall?
AMANDA	Do I look like a 'guy'?
PHIL	Virgin trains, Huggies.

| JULIAN | No. |

| PHIL | We've done loads over the years. |

| JULIAN | You're all woman. |

| WES | You should write a book, pal! |

| PHIL | Oh, no. *You're* the writer. |

| AMANDA | It was rhetorical, actually. But thanks anyway. |

| WES | I love Rik Mayall! Always have. We should have got him. He'd have just *done* this for us – in one. Found the names. Made it funny. |

| DINO | It is funny. |

| LEONIE | Very funny. |

| PHIL | Very very funny. |

| WES | I wonder if that's why Rik Mayall spelt his name with a 'K'. |

| DINO | What? |

| WES | To make it funnier. |

| AMANDA | 'Guys'. It's so horribly American. |

| LEONIE | He'd still have a 'K' in it even if he spelt it the normal way. |

| WES | What? |

| LEONIE | 'Rick' with a 'c', has a 'k'. |

| WES | Yeah but . . . oh, you know what I mean? |

| AMANDA | And sexist. Like girls don't exist. |

PHIL   I suppose it does make it more memorable. 'Rik'!

DINO   You're not going to forget Rik Mayall.

LEONIE   Which one's Rik Mayall?

WES   *The Young Ones.* (*Remembering she's too young.*)
              Oh, yeah.

JULIAN   (*to* AMANDA) The one that gets me is
                          'no worries'.

DINO   So, are we changing it, or what?

AMANDA   That's Australian not American.

JULIAN   It's still annoying. 'No worries. No
                          worries.'

LEONIE   What do you think?

JULIAN   You must have some worries.

WES   'Keswick' Road?

DINO   It's not funnier.

JULIAN   Everyone's got some worries.

AMANDA   Especially Australians, I'd have
                          thought.

JULIAN   Yeah.

AMANDA   Should I work in this bar or this bar?

WES   'Kilmarnock Avenue.'

DINO   Not funnier.

WES   It's got a 'K' in it.

DINO   So, has 'shut the fuck up!'

LEONIE   Guys!

AMANDA   If she says 'guys' again, I really think
                                I'm going to have to say something.

JULIAN   You haven't changed.

                (PHIL *picks up his phone.* LEONIE *presses the
                talkback.*)

LEONIE   I think we're going to leave it as it is, guys.

AMANDA   Okay.

                (LEONIE *takes her finger off the talkback.*)

JULIAN   You really told her!

AMANDA   (*playfully*) Shut up!

WES   (*to* PHIL) Can I get another Stella?

PHIL   (*aware of the Americanism*) Can we 'get' another
                Stella?

WES   (*to* PHIL) Chilled!

PHIL   Chilled.

JULIAN   I see you're finally leaving
                                Eastenders then?

AMANDA   I've left.

DINO   Maybe we should try it in an accent?

WES   What accent?

                (PHIL *puts his phone down.*)

AMANDA   I wanted to do other things.

JULIAN	Like not work for five years and then present something about hospitals at nine in the morning?
AMANDA	Hence the voice-overs. That's where the big money is, right?
JULIAN	It was.
WES	Well, if it's meant to be the Cotswolds . . . (*He looks at* LEONIE.)
JULIAN	As you know.
WES	Where is that? Yorkshire?
DINO	It's Oxfordshire. You Scots git!
WES	So, what's the accent like in Oxfordshire?
PHIL	Oxford-y.
LEONIE	Isn't it all, "ooh, arr"?
WES	(*with distaste*) We don't want that.
LEONIE	I thought the Cotswolds was Gloucestershire . . .
DINO	And Worcestershire. And Warwickshire. It's big.
PHIL	It st-r-etches. (*They all look at him.*) Sorry.
WES	What about Birmingham? Birmingham's funny. Ask if they can do Birmingham.
PHIL	Julian can do Birmingham.
WES	What are you, his agent?
PHIL	We go back a long way. He's told me a lot over the years about . . . all sorts.
WES	In fifty-two different voices?

DINO	Fifty-one!
	(LEONIE *presses the talkback button.*)
LEONIE	We're just talking about accents in here. Can you guys do a Birmingham accent?
JULIAN	This 'guy' can. (*To* AMANDA.) What about this 'guy'?
AMANDA	I should be able to with a surname like mine!
LEONIE	(*after a thought*) Oh. Yes! Ha, ha!
WES	Let's try that, then.
AMANDA	But actually I . . .
PHIL	'No argument.' Take five. Birmingham version.
WES	And then can we go, yeah?
	(*The recording begins again.*)
AMANDA	(*bad Birmingham accent*) We've gone too far!
JULIAN	(*Birmingham accent*) We have *not* gone too far!
AMANDA	We have! Look! That was Bourton Road and Bourton Road is after Blockley Road not before it!
	(LEONIE'S *phone goes.*)
LEONIE	Ooh, sorry!
JULIAN	You've got the map upside down!
AMANDA	It's called orienteering!
LEONIE	(*on phone*) Hi, Jenny. Hi!
JULIAN	It's the next left.
AMANDA	So, you know more than the map?

JULIAN   Perhaps there's a mistake on it.

LEONIE   Oh!

              (PRESTON *enters with the Stella.*)

AMANDA   Yeah, they probably deliberately put mistakes on
              maps to make driving more exciting!

PRESTON   (*passes the Stella to* WES) Dred.

LEONIE   You're kidding!

              (JULIAN *grunts.*)

AMANDA   Let's ask this man.

JULIAN   It's the next left!

AMANDA   Excuse me, which way is Blockley Road?

WES   That's a much better beer.

JULIAN   (*rural accent*) Oh, you've gone way past it, love.
              It's . . .

AMANDA   (*very self-satisfied*) That's all I wanted to know . . .

LEONIE   Of course.

JULIAN   Stop gloating!

AMANDA   I'm not gloating

JULIAN   You are!

AMANDA   I'm not!

JULIAN   You are!

AMANDA   Am not!

JULIAN   Are!

AMANDA   Not!

JULIAN   (*voice-over voice*) The new VM Vogel has Sat Nav
           fitted as standard. It gets you there – no argument!

           (PHIL *presses the talkback.*)

WES   Brilliant! Can we keep that improv?

PHIL   Yeah, I can trim it elsewhere – take a few breaths
           out.

DINO   Doesn't matter if we can't.

WES   I think we've got two really good versions now.

           (PHIL *takes his finger off the talkback.*)

AMANDA   (*to* JULIAN) So . . .

WES   (*to* LEONIE) What?

AMANDA   Can we go?

LEONIE   That was Jenny. The client won't go to thirty.

DINO   What?

WES   You're joking?

LEONIE   No.

WES   Shit-arse!

           (AMANDA *is seeing the heads in hands on the
           other side of the screen.*)

JULIAN   That looks nasty!

DINO   (*to* LEONIE) We've got to *cut* ten seconds?

JULIAN   (*to* AMANDA) Maybe Leonie didn't
                   like your accent.

AMANDA   (*to* JULIAN) It wasn't that bad, was it?

WES   We just got a really good one too! The accents
                    were a masterstroke!

DINO   I thought this was all sorted out.

AMANDA   Julian?

LEONIE   Can't we just go back to the twenty second version?

WES   We never actually wrote a twenty second version.

AMANDA   Jules?!

JULIAN   It was good.

WES   Piss-arse.

PHIL   Any more refreshments for anyone?

AMANDA   Really good?

JULIAN   Well . . . No!

AMANDA   (*hitting him playfully*) Bastard!

WES   I'll have another Stella.

DINO   You haven't finished that one.

WES   Well, I want another one! What are you, my wife?

AMANDA   You know I can't do accents.

JULIAN   I do now!

LEONIE   (*glancing into the booth*) They seem to be getting
                    on well.

WES   Yeah, what's going on in there?

PHIL   Errr . . . Dino?

(AMANDA *looks into the box again.*)

AMANDA	God! What's going on in there?
DINO	I'm fine.
PHIL	Leonie?
JULIAN	God knows!
AMANDA	He's a bit scary – that Irish one.
LEONIE	I'll wait.
JULIAN	He's Scottish.
AMANDA	Told you I was no good at accents!
LEONIE	No. Actually, could you get the menus for lunch?
PHIL	Sure.

(LEONIE *presses the talkback.* PHIL *picks up the phone. The boys look at the script.*)

LEONIE	Guys, we've just heard we've got to cut ten seconds.
JULIAN	Ouch!
PHIL	(*into the phone*) Could we have some menus please?
JULIAN	Do you need us to help?
PHIL	(*into the phone*) And another Stella.
LEONIE	We'll have a stab first.
PHIL	Thanks.
JULIAN	If you're sure.
LEONIE	You guys kick back in there, yeah?

JULIAN   No worries!

            (LEONIE *releases the talkback and sits back in her seat.*)

WES   I really liked that Birmingham one too.

DINO   Have you ever been to Birmingham?

WES   Yeah. It's alright. Why?

DINO   Because I don't think Ms Birmingham has been to Birmingham.

PHIL   Not the best accent I've heard.

LEONIE   I'm hopeless with accents. As far as I'm concerned, people either talk like me or they don't.

            (*They look at her.*)

WES   Sounded fine to me.

LEONIE   Well, it doesn't matter. We've got to do *this* now.

            (PHIL *sits back.* WES, LEONIE *and* DINO *bury their heads in the script.*)

AMANDA   Bit of a cock up, then?

JULIAN   Yeah. (*A pause.*) So, how's Martin?

AMANDA   Don't start!

DINO   (*to* WES *and* LEONIE) We could lose the first three speeches.

JULIAN   Well?

AMANDA   Not here. Not now.

WES   Come in on, 'You've got the map upside down'?

JULIAN   They're not listening. We're not 'up'.
                    This'll take them ages.

AMANDA   I'm not talking about . . .

WES   Nah.

JULIAN   What?

AMANDA   That. Any of that.

JULIAN   Why not?

LEONIE   Why not?

AMANDA   There's nothing to say.

WES   We lose the whole sense of the couple arguing then.

JULIAN   There's everything to say.

AMANDA   Look! Don't think this isn't a
                    nightmare for me too.

WES   We've got to know they're arguing.

AMANDA   I couldn't believe it when I walked in
                    and saw you!

DINO   Keep it in.

JULIAN   Yeah, you'd think we might've
                    bumped into each other by now really.

AMANDA   Ummm. At some BBC party or awards
                    'do'. Or something.

JULIAN   Yeah. 'Cos I move in those circles.

LEONIE   We've got to lose something.

AMANDA   Well, somewhere!

WES   Well, not that!

AMANDA   Things have gone well. What can I say?

WES   She could not say all the road names.

AMANDA   Don't give me a hard time about it.
                                That's the business. Some people get
                                there; some people don't.

JULIAN   Simple as that?

LEONIE   Yes.

AMANDA   Yes.

WES   No one in their right mind knows where those
            places are anyway.

JULIAN   I'm happy for you.

AMANDA   Good!

JULIAN   Happy you 'got there'.

LEONIE   Okay.

JULIAN   It just wasn't easy seeing you on TV
                                three nights a week, months after we
                                split up. And with the omnibus at
                                weekends.

AMANDA   You didn't have to watch.

LEONIE   What about the 'orienteering' line?

AMANDA   And it's four nights a week now.

JULIAN   I know that! But *then* it was three.
                                Back then.

PHIL   It's a bit ABC-1, isn't it?

JULIAN   Wednesday was the one night I
                                relished. Because there was no

chance of seeing you on BBC 1 and
being reminded of all that . . .

DINO   It's gone.

JULIAN   . . . stuff!

AMANDA   Well, what was I supposed to do?
                          Turn it down? (*Miming a phone.*)
                          "The job of a lifetime? Oh, no, I'd
                          better not, Griselda. Jules might
                          watch it and I don't want to risk
                          hurting his feelings."

LEONIE   It's not easy, is it?

JULIAN   It wasn't just about seeing you
                          succeed.

DINO   No.

JULIAN   It wasn't just about not being with you.

WES   Shit!

JULIAN   It was the memory of what we did to her.

AMANDA   Don't talk about that.

DINO   How much have we lost?

AMANDA   It's in the past.

LEONIE   Not enough.

AMANDA   Forgotten. Shut away.

DINO   Ai! Ai! Ai!

AMANDA   That's how we deal with it. How we
                          dealt with it.

LEONIE   What about . . . ?

AMANDA   How everyone deals with it. That . . .

LEONIE   What about . . .

AMANDA   . . . awful . . .

LEONIE   . . . 'they probably deliberately put mistakes on
            maps to make driving more exciting'?

WES   I'm not losing that! It's the only joke in the whole
            script!

AMANDA   Anyway there are listings magazines,
                           aren't there?

LEONIE   It's not very funny though.

JULIAN   What?

WES   What?!

AMANDA   You could have avoided *Eastenders*
                           easily enough.

JULIAN   Plenty of people *do* now.

AMANDA   That's uncalled for!

LEONIE   Is it funny?

WES   You've laughed at it every time.

JULIAN   What do you care anyway? You've
                           left.

AMANDA   Yeah, I've left. I chose to move on.
                           That's what people do in life.

JULIAN   Some people.

DINO   We've got to lose something.

AMANDA   Everyone except you, Julian. You've
                           always wallowed in the past. You

	carry it round with you like a broken umbrella.
WES	*That's* a great line! I'm not losing that line!
DINO	Fine.
LEONIE	(*looking up*) Are they alright in there?
JULIAN	Well, forgive me, but I can't just forget things, alright!! I can't just shut them away.
AMANDA	You did at the time.
JULIAN	Well, it turns out now that I can't.

(LEONIE *presses the talkback.*)

LEONIE	(*casually*) Are you alright in there?
JULIAN	Fine!
AMANDA	Just catching up.
LEONIE	Nice one. We're nearly there.
AMANDA	Sure you don't want any help?
LEONIE	Yeah. Thanks, guys.

(*She takes her finger off the talkback.*)

AMANDA	I wish she'd stop saying that!
JULIAN	She probably fancies you.
AMANDA	She's not . . . ?
JULIAN	Swings both ways, according to Phil. Used to anyway. Before she found God. Your type.
WES	We could lose 'Let's ask this man'.

AMANDA   I was just bi-curious.

LEONIE   Yeah. 'Cos then she asks someone.

AMANDA   I know it excited you.

DINO   That's part of the whole male-female thing though,
           isn't it?

JULIAN   Let's not talk about that.

DINO   She's happy to ask a third party; he's not. It's
           funny! That's what those two lines are about –
           basic gender politics!

AMANDA   So, we just get to talk about what you
                  want to talk about.

PHIL   I think you'll have to cut one of them to get it
           down to twenty. Either 'let's ask this man' or (*To*
           WES.) your 'deliberate mistakes' line.

JULIAN   Perhaps we shouldn't talk about
                  anything.

AMANDA   Perhaps not.

DINO   Okay.

JULIAN   Okay.

DINO   Cut mine.

WES   No! Cut mine!

AMANDA   Fine.

WES   Take them both out!

LEONIE   Shall I get a new script printed?

WES   Nah, it's a waste of paper. Just tell them the cuts.
           They've got enough pencils in there.

PHIL   Are you having a go at my pencils? I'm very proud
            of my pencils.

LEONIE   They're great pencils, Pete.

PHIL   Phil.

LEONIE   Phil.

PHIL   I keep them specially sharpened, you know.

LEONIE   That's really . . .

PHIL   Do you know . . .

LEONIE   Weird.

PHIL   I've often wished I could teach a small mouse to
            lie on them on his back.

DINO   What?

PHIL   Like the old bed of nails trick.

LEONIE   What old 'bed of nails' trick?

WES   You don't see that now, do you?

PHIL   Time was you couldn't move for little, wiry blokes
            lying on a bed of nails somewhere in their pants.

LEONIE   What bed of nails?

DINO   It used to be in all the circuses.

PHIL   Many moons ago.

WES   They still have something similar in Lewisham –
            but you only get to lay on the nails the once.

LEONIE   (to WES and DINO) D'you want to tell them the
            changes?

DINO	I'll do it.
WES	How we doin' for time?
LEONIE	Not brilliant.

(DINO *puts his finger on the talkback button.*)

DINO	Okay. Julian and Amanda?
AMANDA	Yes!

(PRESTON *enters.* WES *holds out his hand to* PRESTON. PRESTON *hands him a Stella then gives* LEONIE *the menus.*)

LEONIE	(*to* PRESTON) Oh, thank you!
PRESTON	My pleasure.
PHIL	(*wanting* PRESTON *to leave*) Er . . . thank you.
PRESTON	My bad.
DINO	Cut the place names line after 'Look!'
AMANDA	Not because I went wrong?
DINO	No.
WES	No!
LEONIE	No!
DINO	Take out 'It's called orienteering'.
JULIAN	It is a bit ABC-1 that, isn't it?
LEONIE	That's just what Pete said!
PHIL	Jesus!
LEONIE	Pete, please! (*Cheekily.*) Were you listening?

JULIAN	No, no! We were . . . No.
PRESTON	(*to* PHIL) D'you want your usual?
PHIL	Yeah, chicken and ham from Shenley's.
DINO	And then cut the 'deliberate mistakes' line.
LEONIE	(*to* PHIL) I thought you were a vegetarian?
PHIL	No.
AMANDA	Oh, I love that line!
WES	Thank you.
DINO	We can put it back if we're under.
LEONIE	We've all got to kill our babies!
DINO	And cut 'Let's ask this man' and the second, 'It's the next left' .
JULIAN	Are we keeping the improv?
DINO	(*to* WES) Are we keeping the improv?
LEONIE	Keep the improv.
PHIL	Keep the improv.
	(PHIL *takes his finger off the talkback.*)
PRESTON	(*to* PHIL) Shall I come back for the other orders?
WES	(*to* PRESTON) Yeah.
	(PRESTON *starts to go.*)
PRESTON	(*to* PHIL) What about the voices?
	(PHIL *presses the talkback.*)
PHIL	Did you want any lunch in there?

LEONIE	Gotta do this!
AMANDA	Ooh, no!
JULIAN	No, thanks. Any other cuts? That doesn't look like ten seconds to me.
WES	What?
JULIAN	It doesn't look like you've taken ten seconds out.
WES	Well, just do it quicker, then!
PHIL	(*releasing the talkback*) Okay?
WES	I think we know what ten seconds looks like. Cheeky fucker!
PHIL	Right. (*To* LEONIE.) Will I call this, 'take one'?
WES	After twenty years in this bloody business, I think I know what . . .
LEONIE	(*interrupting*) Yeah. Keep everything we've done but this is now 'take one'.
DINO	(*irritated*) After thirty-nine minutes!
WES	Thank you, John Motson.
	(AMANDA *is waving.*)
PHIL	Amanda?
AMANDA	With the accents?
DINO/WES	No!
	(*They both pick up menus.*)
PHIL	This is Vogel No Argument – twenty second version . . .

LEONIE   We're looking at an over-run.

PHIL   . . . take one!

           (*The recording begins again.*)

AMANDA   We've gone too far!

JULIAN   We have *not* gone too far!

AMANDA   We have! Look!

JULIAN   You've got the map upside down! It's the next
           left!

AMANDA   So, you know more than the map?

JULIAN   Perhaps there's a mistake on it.

AMANDA   Excuse me, which way is Blockley Road?

JULIAN   (*rural accent*) Oh, you've gone way past it, love.
           It's . . .

AMANDA   That's all I wanted to know . . .

JULIAN   Stop gloating!

AMANDA   I'm not gloating!

JULIAN   You are!

AMANDA   I'm not!

JULIAN   (*voice-over voice*) The new VM Vogel has Sat Nav
           fitted as standard. It gets you there – no argument!

LEONIE   Great!

DINO   How long?

PHIL   Eighteen secs.

LEONIE   Ten seconds shorter.

WES   We need that 'deliberate mistakes' line.

DINO   I didn't miss it.

WES   It's crying out for it!

LEONIE   I didn't miss it.

AMANDA   What are they saying?

JULIAN   It's probably too short now.

WES   The whole thing only works if that line's in!

LEONIE   Put that back we'll have to cut something else.

WES   It's fuckin' pivotal!

JULIAN   What are you doing after this then?

PHIL   I think you need it.

WES   Thank you! At least someone in here's on my wavelength!

AMANDA   I've got to get to this rehearsal.

LEONIE   So, we'll put it back in?

JULIAN   We need to talk.

WES   Yes.

AMANDA   You do; I don't.

JULIAN   Well, Where does *that* leave us?

AMANDA   There is no 'us'.

           (LEONIE *reaches for the talkback button.*)

LEONIE   Guys, can we try putting back in the 'deliberate mistakes' line?

JULIAN	Right.
AMANDA	I'm going to need a new script soon.
LEONIE	Shall I type one up?
WES	We're practically there. Come on!

(PHIL *presses the talkback.*)

PHIL	Happy to go again?

(JULIAN *and* AMANDA *nod.* DINO *and* WES *pick up their menus again.*)

DINO	And try . . . can they hear me?
PHIL	Uh-huh.
JULIAN	They can.
AMANDA	Yes.
DINO	Try and keep up that sense of them being a couple – I think we've lost that a bit. You really had it at first. It seems to have gone a bit.
AMANDA	Okay.
JULIAN	Yep.
WES	Good call, that, actually.
PHIL	Okay, this is . . .
WES	Yeah. A couple . . . can they hear me?
PHIL	Uh-huh.
AMANDA	They can.
WES	A couple who've been together too long, you know?. They were falling out of love a long time

ago . . . maybe started 'swinging' but that all went tits up – literally! And now they're miles apart.

DINO   And lost.

WES   And lost.

LEONIE   And tense.

DINO   That's in the writing.

PHIL   Okay. No Argument – take . . .

WES   And don't forget that extra line's back in.

DINO   And keep the pace up.

AMANDA   Pace or energy?

DINO   Both!

WES   Keep everything up!

JULIAN   We'll try our damnedest!

PHIL   No Argument – take . . .

WES   Oh, and don't do the end-line . . . errr . . . Julian. We can do that separately later.

        (PHIL *turns, taking his finger off the talkback.*)

PHIL   We haven't actually got a timing on the whole read yet.

WES   Oh, yeah. Do it! For the timing.

JULIAN   Can't hear you!

        (WES *presses the talkback.*)

WES   Do it! For the timing. And then we'll do a few 'wild' afterwards.

JULIAN   Okay.

PHIL   Right. Everyone set? This is 'No Argument': Take
             Two . . .

             (*The recording begins again. Now it's really
             tense.*)

AMANDA   We've gone too far!

JULIAN   We have *not* gone too far!

AMANDA   We have! Look! (AMANDA *breaks off.*) Actually,
             can I have a map to hit?

PHIL   I can put that on later.

AMANDA   It would really help though. I think she would hit
             the map at that point and it would affect the voice,
             you know?

PHIL   Sure. Do you want to hit your script?

AMANDA   Okay.

PHIL   Just try it now for us.

             (AMANDA *hits her script.*)

WES   It sounds like someone hitting their script.

PHIL   Try two pages together.

             (AMANDA *hits her script.*)

WES   That sounds like someone hitting two pages
             together.

AMANDA   What about the paper?

DINO   Yeah, can she borrow his paper?

LEONIE   Gotta do this, guys!

DINO   Okay.

PHIL   Let's just hear the paper . . .

            (AMANDA *hits the folded up paper.*)

WES   Sounds like someone hitting a paper.

DINO   A map's got a certain sound.

WES   Yeah, it sounds . . .

DINO   Mappy.

WES   Mappy.

LEONIE   We're getting really tight for time.

PHIL   I'll put it on in post.

WES   (*earnestly*) Something mappy?

PHIL   Yes. Sorry, Amanda. Is that alright?

AMANDA   It was just a thought. Sorry.

WES   It was a very good thought.

LEONIE   Shall we pick it up?

PHIL   I think we should start again, really.

DINO   Okay, this is the one!

WES   Yeah. And maybe a bit less shouty – it was just getting a bit shouty.

DINO   Less shouty but keep it nice and 'up'.

LEONIE   And tense.

JULIAN   I think we can do that, can't we?

AMANDA   (*cheery*) Yes!

PHIL   No Argument . . . twenty seconds . . . Take Three.

AMANDA   We've gone too far!

JULIAN   We have *not* gone too far!

AMANDA   We have! Look!

JULIAN   You've got the map upside down. It's the next left.

AMANDA   So, you know more than the map?

JULIAN   Perhaps there's a mistake on it.

AMANDA   Yeah, they probably deliberately put mistakes on maps to make driving more exciting.

WES   That's a great line!

            (JULIAN *grunts*.)

AMANDA   Excuse me, which way is Blockley Road?

JULIAN   (*rural accent*) Oh, you've gone way past it, love. It's . . .

AMANDA   That's all I wanted to know . . .

JULIAN   Stop gloating!

AMANDA   I am not gloating.

JULIAN   Yes, you are.

AMANDA   No, I'm not.

            (*A pause.*)

JULIAN   Oh, sorry! I couldn't remember whether we said I was doing the end-line now or not. Sorry!

PHIL   It's fine.

(PHIL *turns round, releasing the talkback.*)

WES   How was that for time?

PHIL   Sixteen.

DINO   Which leaves us four for the end-line and effects.

JULIAN   (*to* AMANDA) Sorry. I got confused.
                          What with . . . Everything.

AMANDA   'S fine. You can always do it without me.

DINO   (*to* LEONIE) Happy?

LEONIE   I think so.

(PHIL *presses the talkback.*)

PHIL   We're pretty happy in here. Happy in there?

AMANDA   Yes.

JULIAN   Yes.

(PHIL *turns round, releasing the talkback.*)

PHIL   I think we should do the end-line now and then I
           can patch one together for you.

LEONIE   I'll call Jenny and get her ready to listen down the
           line.

(*She reaches for her phone.*)

AMANDA   (*to* JULIAN) Does that mean I can go?

JULIAN   Probably. You'd better ask.

(AMANDA *waves.* PHIL *catches the wave.*)

PHIL   (*ironically*) Did you want something?

AMANDA	Does that mean I'm free? I'm very happy to stay, obviously, if you need me but . . .

(LEONIE *now has her phone in her hand.*)

LEONIE	We really need to get clearance from the client, Amanda.

AMANDA	Yes, of course.

WES	She should be here.

LEONIE	But step out if you want to while Julian does the end-line for us.

(LEONIE *dials.*)

AMANDA	I'll just make a few calls. Are you sure that's okay?

LEONIE	Yes, of course.

AMANDA	Great.

(AMANDA *starts to pick up her bag.*)

WES	Obviously, we'd rather you stayed so we've got something nice to look at while old fifty-one-voice Julian works his limited magic, you beautiful, sexy, unattainable creature, you!

AMANDA	Cheeky!

(AMANDA *leaves the booth.*)

WES	I thought they couldn't hear me then!

LEONIE	(*into her phone*) It's Leonie. Is Jenny free to listen?

WES	Shite!

PHIL	(*to* DINO) So, we'll just get a few wild?

WES	Shite! She heard what I said?
DINO	Yeah. So did he!
WES	Och, that doesn't matter.
LEONIE	*Still* in a meeting?
DINO	Can he give us two or three on the bounce?
PHIL	Let's just do one first, for timing.
DINO	Okay.
LEONIE	(*into phone*) Can you just let her know we're seconds away here?
	(PHIL *presses the talkback.*)
PHIL	(*to* JULIAN, *sensitively*) Everything alright?
JULIAN	Fine. Thanks, Phil. Yeah. Fine.
PHIL	Okay. Just give us one for timing, matey.
JULIAN	Okay, matey.
PHIL	End-line . . .
LEONIE	(*into phone*) About five minutes?
PHIL	One.
LEONIE	(*into phone*) Okay, bye.
JULIAN	(*voice-over voice*) The new VM Vogel has Sat Nav fitted as standard. It gets you there – no argument!
PHIL	Two seconds.
WES	Perfect for time.
DINO	I thought that was good all round.

PHIL   Leonie?

LEONIE   Sorry. I wasn't listening. Can he do it again?

PHIL   And – take two. Listening version.

JULIAN   (*voice-over voice*) The new VM Vogel has Sat Nav
               fitted as standard. It gets you there – no argument!

LEONIE   Great.

PHIL   Shall I put one together?

WES   Yep.

LEONIE   Yeah. (*To* DINO.) Don't you think?

DINO   Actually, can we just try one . . . Can he hear me?

PHIL   Yep. I'll leave it up.

DINO   Can we just try one where you hit the word 'new'
               a bit more?

JULIAN   Sure.

WES   Good call, that. *Very* good call!

PHIL   Okay. End-line . . . take three.

JULIAN   (*voice-over voice*) The *new* VM Vogel has Sat Nav
               fitted as standard. It gets you there – no argument!

DINO   I think that's better.

WES   (*nodding his head*) We've got to know it's 'new'.

PHIL   If we hear the word 'new' too much though do we
               not risk deflecting from the Sat Nav?

DINO   True.

WES   Yeah.

PHIL   (*to* JULIAN) So just a bit less on 'new', matey.

JULIAN   Okay. And it is 'Vogel', isn't it?

WES   As opposed to . . . ?

JULIAN   Well, if we're going for the real German, it's
            'Vurgel.'

WES   Is it?

JULIAN   It means 'bird'.

LEONIE   Does it?

PHIL   Yeah. It's in The Magic Flute. Papageno charms
            the birds from the trees with his little pipes. (*Hums
            the tune.*) 'Die Vogelen . . .'

LEONIE   Wicked.

JULIAN   So . . . ?

WES   'Vogel'.

LEONIE   Keep it English.

JULIAN   And less stress on 'new'?

WES   That's the one.

PHIL   End-line . . . four.

DINO   This is the one.

JULIAN   (*voice-over voice – slower*) The new VM Vogel
            has Sat Nav fitted as standard. It gets you there –
            no argument!

DINO   How was that for time?

PHIL   Three. It's spreading.

DINO   I think we should lose that beat.

LEONIE	What beat?
DINO	Before 'no argument'.
WES	I like that beat.
DINO	I just think 'It gets you there no argument' is better than, 'it gets you there – beat – no argument'.
PHIL	It would be better for the timing.
	(DINO *presses the talkback*.)
DINO	Can you lose the beat, Julian?
JULIAN	Sorry?
DINO	So that there isn't such a beat before 'no argument'.
JULIAN	Run it together?
DINO	No. There should be a little pause.
PHIL	A 'caesura'.
WES	What?
PHIL	That's what it's called. A little beat – a ceasura.
WES	Right.
DINO	(*to* JULIAN) But not a beat.
JULIAN	There's a hyphen on the page.
DINO	Yeah, but it's a hyphen; not a full stop.
PHIL	I could always tighten the gap this end.
LEONIE	(*shaking her head*) We'll hear it, won't we?

PHIL   You won't.

DINO   Let's just try and get it naturally. Quickly! We're
            nearly there!

PHIL   Okay. Five.

JULIAN   (*voice-over voice*) The new VM Vogel has Sat Nav
            fitted as standard. It gets you there no argument!

            (*The talkback is now down.*)

WES   That just sounds weird now.

DINO   Less 'clever-clever', though.

WES   Weird, though!

PHIL   I can tighten that gap from the previous take.

WES   We need the beat!

LEONIE   (*to* PHIL) That's what we should do. Tighten the
            gap from the previous take.

PHIL   Wilco.

LEONIE   So, have we got it?

WES   Yep!

LEONIE   Dino?

DINO   I think so but . . . d'you not think it sounds a bit
            posh?

WES   I'm from Scotland – to me, anyone sounds 'posh'.

LEONIE   You want to try something more 'street'?

DINO   Yeah, a bit rougher.

WES   We haven't got time, have we?

(LEONIE *checks her watch.*)

LEONIE   Jenny'll be free now. But we've still got ten
            minutes.

PHIL   It'll take me five to put it together with effects and
            everything . . .

DINO   And the tighten on that beat.

PHIL   And the tighten on that beat.

WES   Well, let's just quickly try one more then.

DINO   We've got to get it right!

            (LEONIE *presses her talkback.*)

LEONIE   Julian. We just want to try one that's a bit more
            'street'.

JULIAN   With an accent?

LEONIE   More dead-pan, really.

WES   Like Stephen Slaney.

JULIAN   Really?

DINO   Well, just more casual.

WES   He's your mate down the pub rather than your
            dad, you know?

LEONIE   It's just sounding a bit 'dad-ish'.

JULIAN   Ha! Okay.

            (PHIL *presses the talkback.*)

PHIL   Take six . . .

JULIAN	(*'Stephen Slaney'/Stephen MacIntosh-like*) The new VM Vogel has Sat Nav fitted as standard. It gets you there – no argument!
LEONIE	I like that.
DINO	I like that. Wes?
WES	Yeah.
LEONIE	(*to* PHIL) Mark that one.
JULIAN	(*apologetic*) I put that beat back in – it just feels natural.
WES	(*to* DINO) Told you!
PHIL	(*to* JULIAN) I can always tighten it later, matey.
DINO	(*to* JULIAN) Is there anything else *you* want to try?
JULIAN	Well . . . I could do it as Sean Connery.
WES	Let's hear the Connery.
JULIAN	Really?
WES	Go on! As we've got you . . .
PHIL	Take seven – Connery version.
JULIAN	(*as Sean Connery*) The new VM Vogel has Sat Nav fitted as standard. It gets you there – no argument!
WES	That's brilliant!
DINO	How does he do that?
LEONIE	Everyone does Sean Connery.
WES	Not like that!
LEONIE	So, d'you want to use that?

WES   No!

DINO   No.

LEONIE   Okay. I think we've got this now.

DINO   Actually, can we just try one that's a bit warmer?

WES   That's what's nice about the Connery, actually.
           It's warm.

DINO   Yeah it's got more . . .

PHIL   Warmth?

DINO   Yeah?

PHIL   (*via talkback*) Julian, we just want to try one
           that's a bit warmer.

JULIAN   Warmer, okay.

DINO   It's just starting to sound a bit detached.

LEONIE   A bit cynical.

DINO   No, no. Not cynical. Just a bit . . . detached.

WES   Yeah. Like a car with Sat Nav as standard isn't
           that fucking exciting, for some reason!

JULIAN   Ri-ight!

DINO   So, could we try one that's a bit more . . . more . . .
           purple?

JULIAN   Purple?

DINO   Yeah. You know. Like you're walking down a
           beach. The waves are lapping gently, there's the
           tiniest curl of spume. You're barefoot. Your feet
           are almost numb from the water, the sun's setting,
           you're lost in your memories of this sad-happy

                    childhood. But, back on the prom, is your VM
                    Vogel.

Leonie   That's so sweet.

Dino   Okay?

Julian   Right.

Phil   So, all that then, matey. Take eight . . .

Julian   (*'purple'*) The new VM Vogel has Sat Nav fitted as
                    standard. It gets you there – no argument!

Dino   Ummm. Not sure. What d'you think?

Wes   No.

Leonie   Okay. So, we like the 'street' one?

Dino   We really like the 'street' one.

Leonie   And you liked take one.

Wes   Yeah.

Dino   Actually, can we hear that one again?

Phil   Take one?

Wes   Take one! (*To* Dino.) Spume?!

                    (Phil *cues up and plays 'take one'.*)

Julian   (*voice-over voice*) The new VM Vogel has Sat-Nav
                    fitted as standard. It gets you there – no
                    argument!

Dino   I think that's the best one.

Leonie   You know, I think it is.

Wes   It's got that beat in it too.

Dino	Yeah. But it's not too long.
Leonie	So, we're going with take one, yeah?
Wes	Yeah.
Dino	Yeah.
Leonie	Okay. So, let's hear it cut together, if we may, Paul.
Phil	Phil.
Leonie	I am so sorry! (*Looking at her notes.*) End-line one and the body of take three – twenty second version.
Phil	Okay.

(PRESTON *enters.*)

Preston	Did anyone want lunch?

(AMANDA *re-enters the booth.*)

Leonie	I think we're nearly done.
Wes	I'll get something and take it back. Saves queuing up in 'Pret', eh?
Preston	Look after those pennies.
Wes	What's that, 'dred'?
Preston	Know what I mean?
Wes	Not often.
Amanda	(*to* JULIAN) All done?
Julian	Pretty much.
Phil	You've got my order.
Preston	Innit?

(PHIL *puts on his headphones and starts to 'mix'.*)

WES   Bacon and egg mayonnaise baguette from
            Shenley's. And a Stella.

PRESTON   Another Stella?

WES   Yes!

PRESTON   (*impressed*) Know what I mean?

            (PRESTON *writes it down on a little pad.*)

AMANDA   (*sitting down*) I don't think I'll be
                        going out there again.

DINO   I'll have a ham and mozzarella ciabatta from
            Antonio's, please. No butter.

JULIAN   Why not?

PRESTON   Yeah, man.

AMANDA   Tess Daly's just come in!

PRESTON   Leonie? Anythink for you, man?

JULIAN   So?

AMANDA   I laid into her in some silly, 'Q and A'
                        thing in the *Mail On Sunday*.

LEONIE   No. I'm not hungry.

PRESTON   Sure?

AMANDA   They misquoted me, of course, but I
                        heard she was really annoyed by it!

JULIAN   Oh.

AMANDA   And Vernon Kay.

LEONIE   Oh, okay then. Can I just have chicken, avocado
                and prawns with mayo and lots of black pepper on
                a wholemeal bap from Shenley's?

AMANDA   Really annoyed!

LEONIE   With some salt and vinegar crisps.

JULIAN   Right.

LEONIE   And a chocolate brownie.

PRESTON   Sweet.

LEONIE   And a rocky road.

JULIAN   Oh, the trials of celebrity!

LEONIE   And a diet coke.

WES   Yeah, don't want to put any weight on, eh?

PRESTON   What about the voices?

JULIAN   Looks like you're stuck with me, then.

                (LEONIE *presses the talkback.*)

LEONIE   D'you want any food, guys?

AMANDA   I'm fine, thanks.

JULIAN   No, thanks.

LEONIE   I'll try Jenny again.

                (PRESTON *leaves.* LEONIE *picks up her mobile and
                dials.* DINO *and* WES *have both picked up
                magazines and are flicking through them.*)

AMANDA   What's happening?

JULIAN   Phil's putting it together and then
                                they'll play it to the client down the

	line. And then we all go our separate ways. Again.
AMANDA	Right.
LEONIE	It's Leonie from MBSTWD and D again. Hi!
JULIAN	So, did you ever . . .
LEONIE	Is Jenny free now?
	(*She holds.*)
JULIAN	. . . did you ever think about me?
AMANDA	Oh, Julian, please!
JULIAN	Please what? Leave it for next time? You know there won't be a 'next time.'
AMANDA	We don't know that.
LEONIE	If you could, that would be great!
JULIAN	Did you ever think about me?
AMANDA	In the last seven years?
JULIAN	Yes.
LEONIE	(*on phone*) Still in a meeting?!
AMANDA	What do you think?
JULIAN	I don't know what to think. I thought I knew seven years ago what you were thinking and doing and then, clearly – Bang! Gone! I didn't.
LEONIE	Could you put a post-it under her nose?
JULIAN	We never even said 'goodbye'.
LEONIE	(*on phone*) Can she call me as soon as she's out?

AMANDA	Well, I thought about you every day.
LEONIE	(*on phone*) Thanks, bye.
JULIAN	You did?
AMANDA	Well, you always used to go on at me about leaving the tap running when I cleaned my teeth. So, I thought about you every day – when I cleaned my teeth. Twice a day. Sometimes three times if I had a strong lunch.
JULIAN	Alright.
AMANDA	It's true. And then I heard your voice on about a thousand and one voice-overs. It was like being contacted from beyond the grave.
JULIAN	If I ever want to contact you from beyond the grave, I hope I'll say a bit more than, 'If anyone can, Canon can'. (*Without doing a voice.*)

(LEONIE *presses the talkback.*)

LEONIE	Guys, just to let you know. We're waiting for the client to ring us back. Shouldn't be long.
JULIAN	Okay.
AMANDA	Fine.
LEONIE	Are you okay in there, yeah?
AMANDA	Yeah.
JULIAN	Fine.
LEONIE	Wicked!

(LEONIE *takes her finger of the talkback and also picks up a magazine.*)

JULIAN   Apart from that?

AMANDA   I thought about you, Jules. You don't go out with someone for five years and then just forget all about them.

JULIAN   And her? Did you think about her?

AMANDA   Of course. Of course I did. Now, can we leave all this for another time?

JULIAN   When?

AMANDA   We'll have a drink next week or something.

JULIAN   But we won't, will we?

WES   I quite fancied that *Stormcracker* until I saw Kurt Russell was in it.

DINO   Yeah, I know. There's something about Kurt Russell, isn't there?

JULIAN   We shouldn't have done it, you know.

AMANDA   Well, we did. Alright? But it's in the past. Dead and buried. Let's leave it that way!

LEONIE   I think he's a good actor, Kurt Russell.

AMANDA   Please!

WES   I'm not denying that. It's just that almost every film he's ever done has been shite. (*Pause.*) Basically, if you see that Kurt Russell's in a film, you know it'll be shite.

AMANDA   So, you have been okay – generally?

JULIAN	(*equally sarcastic*) Brilliant.
LEONIE	He hasn't done badly though – financially.
AMANDA	You haven't done badly though – financially?
JULIAN	Money isn't everything.
WES	Money isn't everything.
AMANDA	It was.
DINO	It is.
LEONIE	I bet he'd make a lovely Dad.
AMANDA	Didn't your mum always say, 'Only people who've got money say it isn't everything'?
JULIAN	Yes. She did.
DINO	(*wistfully*) He's got a lovely daughter.
JULIAN	She did.
WES	And wife.
AMANDA	How is Maureen?
JULIAN	She died.
WES	Lucky bastard!
AMANDA	Jules! I'm so sorry! I had no idea!
WES	But his films are shite!
AMANDA	Oh, God!
LEONIE	*Tango and Cash*?
JULIAN	Not really!

WES	Shite!
AMANDA	What?
JULIAN	She's alive and kicking . . .
LEONIE	*Tequila Sunrise*?
JULIAN	. . . and living in Hatch End.
WES	Which is shite!
AMANDA	You bastard! You shouldn't joke about things like that!
DINO	*Big Trouble In Little China.*
WES	Shite!
JULIAN	It's not been easy, you know, seeing you everywhere, arm-in-arm with 'Martin' . . . and 'Stephen' . . .
AMANDA	(*sighs*) Ohhh! Please!
JULIAN	Watching Stephen rub sun cream into you where I used to rub sun cream into you.
AMANDA	We never went to Antigua.
JULIAN	(*forcefully*) You know what I mean!
AMANDA	Well, you didn't have to read it all.
JULIAN	I couldn't escape it!
LEONIE	*Escape From New York*?
WES	Good shite! But still shite!
DINO	I think you've made your point.

WES   I thank you!

AMANDA   So, I presume you enjoyed reading
                          about the break-ups.

JULIAN   Why?

AMANDA   "She left me for him but he couldn't
                          keep her happy either?"

WES   It must be burning away inside him.

AMANDA   Or him.

LEONIE   What?

WES   That he just wants to do one really good part in a
             really good film instead of just churning out shite!

JULIAN   No.

AMANDA   I don't believe you.

WES   I bet that's what keeps him going. "One day,
             Goldie Hawn, I'll actually do something quite
             good. Something to make you really proud of me."

DINO   There speaks the voice of experience.

AMANDA   If you sat at home, all those years,
                          envying me – don't envy me that.

WES   You what?

AMANDA   The exposure.

DINO   Sounds like you talking.

JULIAN   I didn't.

WES   What are you saying?

JULIAN   I didn't envy you.

AMANDA   Not much.

JULIAN   Not now.

DINO   That you'd be happy if you could create one really
                    good bit of art instead of all this 'shite'.

AMANDA   Oh, come on, Bunny! You always
                             wanted the big TV series, the big film
                             parts, the fame – we both did!

WES   I'm not sure I like what you're saying here, Dino . . .

DINO   No, you wouldn't.

AMANDA   That's why we did what we did.

                    (WES *stands up.*)

WES   Are you saying I've produced nothing but shite
                    all my life?

LEONIE   He's not saying that, Wes.

JULIAN   Well, your priorities change.

DINO   I didn't mean that!

LEONIE   He didn't mean that, Wes.

WES   Well, that's what it fucking sounded like!

                    (WES *pushes* DINO's *foot with his foot.*)

JULIAN   You see what that exposure does to
                             people.

                    (DINO *stands.*)

LEONIE   Boys, please!

JULIAN   And you see what's important.

Wes	You've not done too badly off the back of my shite, you little shite!
Julian	And what you want.
Wes	You and little Miss Stepford at home, there.
Amanda	And what is important?
Dino	Well, you've not done too badly the last few years letting me do all the fucking work while you roll around with your tenth bottle of Stella in your hand!
Amanda	What did you want?
Julian	I wanted you.
Wes	You want to start looking for a new partner? 'Cos you're about to lose this one!
Julian	I wanted you and I wanted her.
Amanda	Don't talk about her!
Dino	And you're about to lose this one!
Leonie	Boys!
	(DINO *and* WES *are nose to nose like angry footballers.*)
Julian	You and her!
Amanda	Stop it, Jules! Please!
	(*During* AMANDA'S *line,* PRESTON *walks in to the booth. The moment is broken.*)
Preston	Oh, sorry, wrong room!
	(PRESTON *leaves.*)
Wes	Come on, then!

LEONIE   Guys!

                (PHIL *takes off his headphones.*)

PHIL   Ready for a listeny-back?

                (*He sees* WES *and* DINO *squaring up to each other. And* LEONIE *standing between them.*)

                Everything alright?

                (PRESTON *enters. Everyone stares at each other in the creatives' side.*)

PRESTON   One ham and mozzarella foccaccia . . . (*He gives* DINO *his sandwich.* JULIAN *and* AMANDA *are still.*) One bacon and egg baguette and another Stella. (*He silently gives* WES *his sandwich.*) One chicken, avocado and prawns with mayo . . . (*He gives her the sandwich.*)

LEONIE   Thanks.

PRESTON   And lots of black pepper on a wholemeal bap . . .

LEONIE   Yes.

PRESTON   And salt and vinegar 'cripps' . . .

                (*And the crisps.*)

LEONIE   Thanks.

PRESTON   And a chocolate brownie . . .

                (*And the brownie.*)

LEONIE   Thanks, Preston.

PRESTON   And a rocky road.

                (*And the rocky road.*)

LEONIE   Yeah, thanks Preston.

PRESTON   And a Diet Coke . . .

LEONIE   Wicked.

             (*He gives her the Coke.*)

PRESTON   Not that you need it.

             (WES *and* DINO *sit down.*)

PHIL   Did you get mine?

PRESTON   Shit, man!

             (PRESTON *rushes out.*)

JULIAN   Don't you regret . . .

             (PHIL *presses the talkback.*)

PHIL   We're just going to have a listeny-back, I think.

AMANDA   Great!

LEONIE   Right!

JULIAN   Excellent!

WES   Sure!

DINO   Cool!

PHIL   Everyone sitting comfortably?

LEONIE   Go for it!

             (PHIL *presses play and everyone sits and listens to
             the advert. It now starts with the noise of a car
             horn, has car sound effects, a map noise, a
             window going down, 'the man' sounds off, a
             lovely fade on the improvised argument and the
             end-line added.*)

AMANDA   *WE'VE GONE TOO FAR!*

JULIAN   *WE HAVE* NOT *GONE TOO FAR!*

AMANDA   *WE HAVE! LOOK!*

JULIAN   *IT'S THE NEXT LEFT.*

AMANDA   *SO, YOU KNOW MORE THAN THE MAP?*

JULIAN   *PERHAPS THERE'S A MISTAKE ON IT.*

AMANDA   *YEAH, THEY PROBABLY DELIBERATELY PUT MISTAKES ON MAPS TO MAKE DRIVING MORE EXCITING!*

            (JULIAN *GRUNTS.*)

AMANDA   *EXCUSE ME, WHICH WAY IS BLOCKLEY ROAD?*

JULIAN   (*RURAL ACCENT*) *OH, YOU'VE GONE WAY PAST IT, LOVE. IT'S . . .*

AMANDA   *THAT'S ALL I WANTED TO KNOW . . .*

JULIAN   *STOP GLOATING!*

AMANDA   *I AM NOT GLOATING.*

JULIAN   *YES, YOU ARE.*

AMANDA   *NO, I'M NOT.*

JULIAN   (*VOICE-OVER-VOICE*) *THE NEW VM VOGEL HAS SAT-NAV FITTED AS STANDARD. IT GETS YOU THERE — NO ARGUMENT!*

WES   Brilliant!

DINO   Really nice!

LEONIE   Good work, Phil!

PHIL   Happy?

DINO	I like the map noise; it was really . . .
PHIL	'Mappy'?
WES	(*earnestly*) Yeah.
DINO	(*earnestly*) But not too 'mappy'.
WES	And that improv works really well – it really lifts it!
JULIAN	Thanks!
AMANDA	Can we go?
LEONIE	(*to* JULIAN *and* AMANDA) Can I just ask you to stay until we've played it to the client?
AMANDA	Oh, yes.
LEONIE	Just in case there's anything she wants to change.
DINO	Sure to be something.
PHIL	Sure to be.
WES	She should fucking be here!
AMANDA	Will it take long?
LEONIE	Seconds.
AMANDA	I really ought to be going.
LEONIE	Literally seconds. I'm just calling her now, Amanda.
	(LEONIE *releases the talkback and picks up her mobile.*)
DINO	It's good.
WES	Not 'shite' then?

DINO   It's good.

PHIL   It's funny.

LEONIE   Very funny!

WES   (*to* DINO) Not shite?

DINO   No!

LEONIE   No! (*Into phone.*) It's Leonie from MBSTWD and D. Is Jenny . . .

AMANDA   (*to* JULIAN) Well, it's been good to see you again.

WES   Not shite?

DINO   Not shite.

JULIAN   (*ironically*) Yeah, we've finally sorted a few things out, eh?

PHIL   It's the improv that really makes it.

DINO   Yeah, I think the body of it works well too.

LEONIE   (*into phone*) Still in a meeting.

WES   Sounds good, Phil.

PHIL   That's why I'm here.

LEONIE   (*into phone*) No, it's switched off. She always switches it off in meetings. Helpfully!

AMANDA   You doing another one today?

JULIAN   Yeah. Got one at two. So . . .

WES   Fancy a quick one or two when we've got the o-kay?

DINO	O-kay. Something I want to talk to you about, actually.
JULIAN	I can't hang about.
DINO	Need to talk to you about.
WES	Sounds ominous.
DINO	That sandwich looks good.

(WES *and* DINO *sit on the sofas and begin leafing through up-market lads' mags.*)

LEONIE	(*into phone*) Could you let her know . . .
AMANDA	Let's hope the client likes it, uh?
LEONIE	(*into the phone*) Oh, she does. (*Beat.*) Yeah, the Japanese, I know. Okay, bye.

(LEONIE *presses the talkback.*)

LEONIE	Sorry, guys, our client is still in a meeting. Are you okay to hang on for a little mo?
JULIAN	Sure.
AMANDA	It won't be too long?
LEONIE	They said she'd call me back within the next two or three mins.

(LEONIE *takes her finger off the talkback.*)

JULIAN	So, that'll be another half an hour, then.
DINO	(*to* LEONIE) You're looking at an over-run.
LEONIE	Not necessarily.
AMANDA	Not necessarily.

WES   She's bound to find something wrong though.

DINO   That's the good thing about leaving the improv in.
           If she doesn't like the ad, we can offer to take that
           out.

PHIL   I love that improv – it works really well. (WES *and*
           DINO *look at him.*) In conjunction with the script,
           obviously.

           (*A pause.*)

AMANDA   So, are you with anyone?

JULIAN   Not at this moment in time, no.

AMANDA   Oh.

PHIL   Maybe she'll want to take out the 'deliberate
           mistakes' line.

WES   She'd better fucking not!

DINO   Glad to see you're open to suggestions.

WES   I haven't quite forgiven you yet.

           (PRESTON *enters with* PHIL'S *sandwich. He hands it
           to him.*)

PHIL   Ah!

PRESTON   Know what I mean?

PHIL   Thanks Preston.

PRESTON   (*looking at* LEONIE) Want me to stay in and learn
           more about the desk?

PHIL   I'll just see you for post.

PRESTON   Right. Sweet. Laters.

           (PRESTON *leaves and* PHIL *sets about his sandwich.*)

AMANDA   But there have been . . . women?

JULIAN   Yeah, there have been women.

LEONIE   Let's hope Jenny likes it.

PHIL   She should like it.

WES   She should. It's bloody good!

PHIL   With just that hint of Tarantino.

WES   Yes!

DINO   Yes!

AMANDA   But no one now?

JULIAN   Not at this moment in time, no.

              (LEONIE'S *phone goes.*)

LEONIE   (*into phone*) It's Leonie. Oh, hi, mum! Look can I
              call you back in ten mins? It's just . . .

AMANDA   No ex-wife?

JULIAN   No.

AMANDA   No kids?

JULIAN   No kids.

LEONIE   Really?

AMANDA   Really?

LEONIE   Well, of course I will.

JULIAN   Don't you speak to any of the old
                          gang?

AMANDA   I did at first, yes, but I lost touch.

LEONIE   It has not been six months since I came home!

AMANDA   You do, don't you?

JULIAN   I suppose you do.

LEONIE   Look, can I just . . . ?

AMANDA   I heard there was a Tamsin and then
                            the trail went cold.

JULIAN   It tends to do that when you're not
                            all over the newspapers.

LEONIE   Oh, that's awful!

JULIAN   Anyway, they all got fed up of me
                            talking about you.

LEONIE   Did they?

AMANDA   You didn't tell anyone about what we
                            did?

LEONIE   Only £2.50? Well, that's . . .

JULIAN   No. Of course not.

LEONIE   Did you?

JULIAN   Did *you*?

LEONIE   Yes.

AMANDA   No.

JULIAN   Do you wish we hadn't done it?

AMANDA   You can't ask that!

JULIAN   Why not?

LEONIE   It really hasn't been six months, mum.

AMANDA	Not here.
JULIAN	Then never. You'll be busy. You'll be filming. You'll avoid my calls.
LEONIE	This line's awful.
JULIAN	Do you wish we hadn't done it?
AMANDA	Everything would be different.
LEONIE	You're cutting out . . . Can I . . . ? . . . just . . . bad . . . call . . . back . . . I . . . a . . . I . . .

(*She cuts off the call.*)

PHIL	Naughty!
LEONIE	Well!
JULIAN	Well? Do you or don't you?
AMANDA	Stop bullying me!
JULIAN	This isn't bullying.
AMANDA	I can't talk about it now.
JULIAN	I need to know!
AMANDA	Now?
JULIAN	Yes!

(LEONIE's *phone rings again.*)

LEONIE	(*in one breath*) I can't talk now, I'll call you tonight!
JULIAN	Do you wish we hadn't done it?
AMANDA	That was then.

WES   That could have been Jenny!

DINO   Did you check the caller ID?

LEONIE   No!

JULIAN   Do you wish we hadn't done it?

AMANDA   It doesn't work like that.

DINO   Just check 'received calls'.

JULIAN   So, how does it work?

LEONIE   I don't know how it works.

DINO   (*kindly*) Give it to me.

AMANDA   If we hadn't done what we did,
                              everything would be different.
                              Everything. So, you know . . .

LEONIE   I can just do texts and calls so far.

PHIL   The wonder of the iPhone.

AMANDA   I can't say, I wish we hadn't done it
                              because if we had *not* done it, I
                              wouldn't be where I am now – *who* I
                              am now to say I wish we hadn't. Nor
                              would you.

DINO   (*holding his hand out*) Give it to me!

AMANDA   The whole physical reality would be
                              different.

JULIAN   I know. You'd be a mum . . .

             (LEONIE's *phone goes.*)

JULIAN   . . . and we'd still be together.

LEONIE   (*into phone*) Mum? I'm so sorry. I thought you were going to be my mother.

AMANDA   We don't know that.

LEONIE   Was that you? Sorry.

AMANDA   We can't know that.

LEONIE   Any idea when she'll be free to listen? Okay, bye.

JULIAN   We *would* still be together.

AMANDA   Well, then I'm glad we did what we did!

LEONIE   At last, an answer!

AMANDA   I'm . . .

         (LEONIE *presses the talkback.*)

LEONIE   I'm sorry, guys. We're looking at an over-run. Can you stay?

JULIAN   Sure.

AMANDA   You know I've absolutely got to leave in a quarter of an hour?

LEONIE   I'm sure it won't take that long.

PHIL   Do you want any more drinks in there?

JULIAN   I'm fine. Mand?

AMANDA   Maybe a tea, actually. I think I *need* a tea.

PHIL   I can get you a glass of wine if you want.

AMANDA   Oh! Go on, then.

PHIL   Red or white?

AMANDA   Oh, anything. Red. No, white. No. Yes, white.

PHIL   Matey? Glass of vino?

JULIAN   Not while I'm working, matey, thanks.

AMANDA   You always were so fucking self-righteous!

JULIAN   And you were always a lush waiting to happen!

PHIL   Just the one white wine, then!

              (PHIL *takes his finger off the talkback.*)

WES   What did she just say?

              (PHIL *picks up the phone.*)

AMANDA   Did they hear that?

JULIAN   Yep!

PHIL   (*into phone*) Hi . . .

WES   Have those two got history?

AMANDA   And how much else have they heard?

PHIL   One white wine, one tea, please.

              (PHIL *puts the phone down.*)

JULIAN   Nothing else.

DINO   Sounds like it!

AMANDA   How do you know?

JULIAN   Phil fades us down.

WES   Phil, fade them up!

AMANDA   How much else have they heard??

JULIAN	If he heard anything juicy he'd fade us down.
PHIL	I can't do that.
JULIAN	We go back years.
WES	Why not?
PHIL	It's not ethical.
JULIAN	Almost as far as you and me.
AMANDA	Right.
JULIAN	But, obviously, Phil and I never had to choose whether or not we had a . . .
AMANDA	(*cuts him off*) Jules, please!
WES	Sod that!
JULIAN	What?
PHIL	No! Sorry.
LEONIE	(*to* WES) It's not right!
DINO	Wes!
WES	Come on, Phil!
AMANDA	Look, we both agreed to do it at the time.
JULIAN	It was your final decision though.
AMANDA	It was my body.
WES	Go on, matey!
AMANDA	And anyway, you weren't big enough to decide.

PHIL   No!

AMANDA   Probably in case I ended up blaming
                         you one day – and you couldn't take
                         that responsibility.

JULIAN   But we didn't think hard enough!

AMANDA   What?

WES   You could have just forgotten to fade them down.

AMANDA   We looked at it from every angle.

JULIAN   Did we?

AMANDA   Yes, we did. We said it was too early
                         for a baby.

DINO   Leave it, Wes!

PHIL   I always fade actors down because they can bore
                for England.

WES   But that sounded dead juicy.

AMANDA   We didn't want a baby then.

DINO   Wes!

WES   (*searching the sound desk*) Talk to Daddy.

AMANDA   You certainly didn't want a baby.

                (WES *walks towards the desk and looks for the
                right button.*)

WES   Ah-ha!

                (WES *has found the right slidey thing and 'opens
                up' the studio.*)

AMANDA   I'd just got that long TIE job . . . And
                  you were about to go to Coventry to
                  do errr . . .

JULIAN   *Carousel.*

AMANDA   With . . .

JULIAN   Michael Ball.

AMANDA   Michael Ball.

JULIAN   With a possible West End transfer –
                  that never happened.

AMANDA   And you were down to last the two
                  for Egg in *This Life* and the 'second
                  airman' in *The English Patient*.

WES   I see what you mean.

JULIAN   If only I'd known then that 'down to
                  the last two' is agent-speak for
                  'nowhere bloody near, darling'.

WES   Actors, eh?

AMANDA   Agents, eh?

JULIAN   Yeah.

DINO   Turn them off, Wes!

LEONIE   Yeah, turn them off!

                  (WES *takes his hand off the talkback and walks
                  back to his sofa and picks up a newspaper.* DINO
                  is fiddling with an executive toy. PHIL *munches
                  away on his sandwich.*)

AMANDA   A baby just wasn't part of those
                  plans.

JULIAN   But that child was meant to be.

AMANDA   Nothing is 'meant to be.'

JULIAN   A path was opening up and we
                          played God.

AMANDA   Don't tell me you've got religious
                          now. Is that what this is all about?

JULIAN   Jesus! No! I'm just suddenly haunted
                          by it.

AMANDA   Suddenly?

JULIAN   Yes.

AMANDA   Suddenly?

WES   Bloody hell! They killed this kid!

JULIAN   I don't know why.

DINO   What kid?

AMANDA   You haven't really thought about it
                          'til now?

WES   Eleven years old!

JULIAN   Well . . .

LEONIE   Come on!

WES   For an iPod.

JULIAN   It's been the last few weeks for some
                          reason. Up until then, no. Not really.

WES   In my fucking street!

JULIAN   Weirdly.

WES   Just a baby.

DINO   (*reading over* WES'S *shoulder*) A Peach 120Si.

JULIAN   I think we made a mistake. Then.

DINO   We did that campaign.

JULIAN   And we're paying for it now.

WES   Fucking hell! (*He throws the paper down and picks up a magazine.*)

AMANDA   We took charge of our lives, okay? In just the same way we did every time we used a condom.

WES   Just a kid.

AMANDA   We just made the decision a little later, that's all.

JULIAN   When our child existed!

AMANDA   A sperm exists!

LEONIE   Come on!

JULIAN   That's different.

AMANDA   That's what we said at the time. That's what we said – calmly and rationally. Both of us.

LEONIE   (*at her phone*) Oh, come on!

AMANDA   Jules, they couldn't even tell what sex it was; you decided it was a girl.

JULIAN   I still think it was.

AMANDA   Did you see it?

                (JULIAN *is silent.*)

AMANDA   Did you have it suckered out of you?

(JULIAN *is silent.*)

AMANDA   No! You weren't there. You weren't
                                even there to hold my hand or hold
                                me when it was done.

JULIAN   And I'll never forgive myself for that,
                                Mand.

AMANDA   You were doing a voice-over.

JULIAN   It was a big campaign.

AMANDA   We had money.

JULIAN   Well, we needed more money!

AMANDA   What for? School fees?

(JULIAN *is silent.*)

AMANDA   You could have just said 'no', for once.

JULIAN   I made sure Rachel was there.

AMANDA   Rachel wasn't the father!

JULIAN   I got there as soon as I could.

AMANDA   It was all over by then. All done. The
                                whole thing gone as if by magic!

JULIAN   Maybe if I'd been there, I'd be coping
                                better now.

AMANDA   Maybe if you'd been there, I'd have
                                coped better then! And if you want to
                                know why we split up, Julian, one of
                                the reasons is right there. When I
                                really needed you, *really* needed you,
                                you weren't there. 'Glade' air
                                freshener was more important!

JULIAN	It was 'Air-Wick'.
AMANDA	Whatever it was!!!

(PRESTON *enters. The moment is broken.*)

PRESTON	One white wine . . .
WES	(*looking at his mag*) Kate Moss's nipples are bigger than her tits!
DINO	Can't understand the Kate Moss thing.
AMANDA	Thank you!
PRESTON	And one Early Grey. Milk, one sugar.
LEONIE	Oh, I can.

(*They both look at her.*)

JULIAN	Thanks. Thanks, Preston.

(PRESTON *leaves the booth.*)

WES	Kelly Brook on the other hand . . . or hands.
LEONIE	I don't believe you, Wes!
WES	What? Just cos you're married, you don't stop looking, do you?
LEONIE	Well, you should!
WES	Well, you don't. I asked my dad once, bless him. He was seventy-six at the time. I said to him, 'Dad, when do you stop looking at women?' He said, 'Son, I still look.' Seventy-six. 'Just because,' he said, 'just because you might've bought a beautiful painting, you don't stop going to art galleries, do you?'
DINO	I didn't know your dad liked art.

WES   He didn't.

                    (LEONIE *leans forward to press the talkback.*)

LEONIE   (*to* JULIAN *and* AMANDA) Really sorry, guys. We're
                    still waiting for the client to ring us.

AMANDA   Still in a meeting?

LEONIE   Yeah. With the Japanese.

AMANDA   Maybe the sushi's poisoned her!

LEONIE   (*not getting it*) Oh, no. I don't think so. Anyway,
                    she shouldn't be long. Sorry.

                    (*She takes her finger off the button.*)

AMANDA   (*to* JULIAN) Don't you think I haven't
                                    been haunted by it too?

JULIAN   You didn't look haunted in *Hello*!

LEONIE   How does it work?

AMANDA   I think about it all the time.

WES   What?

AMANDA   All the time.

LEONIE   Sat Nav? How does it work?

AMANDA   I think maybe that was my chance.
                                    My chance to be a mother.

WES   Well . . .

AMANDA   And I chose this instead.

WES   . . . there's a satellite up there somewhere. And it
                    knows where you are.

AMANDA   *We* chose this.

WES   And it activates the voice thing and bingo!

JULIAN   You look great, by the way.

LEONIE   But how does the little lady know where you are?

AMANDA   Thank you. So do you.

WES   What little lady?

AMANDA   (*to herself*) I wonder if I can go to the
                                ladies . . .

LEONIE   Is she watching your car? On a camera or
                something?

                (AMANDA *starts to wave at the box.*)

PHIL   (*to* LEONIE) I think Amanda wants you . . .

                (LEONIE *presses the talkback.*)

LEONIE   Hi!

AMANDA   Just going to the loo, is that okay?

LEONIE   Defo.

                (LEONIE *releases the talkback.* AMANDA *leaves the
                booth.*)

WES   She's not actually watching you. No one's
                watching you, are they?

DINO   I don't know. I don't know how it works.

PHIL   It doesn't always.

WES   (*to* LEONIE) Perhaps God's watching you – and he
                decides to send the good people the right way –
                via Guildford – and the evil people the wrong
                way – via Gdansk.

PHIL   Actually, it's all on a chip, activated by a signal
            from the satellite. Just like your phone, really. We
            recorded all the directions with Joanna Lumley in a
            session in here, ironically.

WES   That is ironic, Phil.

PHIL   I thought so.

WES   (*to* DINO) You're right though. It is shite, all this. I
            mean, what are we doing selling a car anyway?

LEONIE   Let's hope it's more than one car!

DINO   Yeah. Thousands of cars hopefully.

LEONIE   If we want to keep the account.

WES   But the damage that cars are doing to the world.

DINO   People are going to buy them anyway; we don't
            make any difference.

WES   Well, if we don't make any difference, laddo, why
            are we doing it? We must make a difference.

LEONIE   Of course we do.

PHIL   Of course you do.

WES   Yeah. We make a difference. Look at the difference
            we've made. We've made people fat, we've made
            people lazy, we've made people greedy.

DINO   We haven't done that!

WES   We've made shite things look glamorous. Un-do-
            without-able.

PHIL   Is that strictly a word?

WES   Fabric softeners, kitchen towels, air fresheners,
            plug-in air-fresheners, fruit corners, Yakult, DFS,
            KFC, Sky . . . do you really need any of it? No

wonder we've been rubbish at football for so long; we've made shopping for shite our national sport!

DINO   That's our skill.

WES   Well, whoop-de-doo!

PHIL   It's a fine skill!

WES   Bollocks! We offer people happiness but . . .

LEONIE   That's a good thing!

WES   Yeah, being happy is a good thing but we always suggest it's only a drink away, a spray of perfume away, a tin of fuckin' Campbells Meatballs away. "Have these things – buy these things and you'll be happy."

DINO   Well, maybe people are happier when they have those things.

PHIL   Not after they have a tin of meatballs, they're not!

LEONIE   I quite like those meatballs. (*Beat.*) In a common sort of way.

WES   But . . . as soon as they get the happy-making thing, we show them another happy-making thing and tell them they need that too. And another. And another. All we're saying is that they'll never actually be happy. Not until they have everything – which is impossible! In fact, real happiness is not having things. Real happiness is simplicity. Solitude. Peace.

PHIL   Only people who have everything say that happiness is about not having things.

WES   Yeah, 'cos they realise it's all shite. We've all got to have the thing that's a little bit better than the thing we didn't realize wasn't good enough before.

LEONIE   That's clever. (*Beat.*) Can you say that again?

WES   (spelling it out) We all have to have the thing
           that's a little bit better than the thing we didn't
           realise wasn't good enough before.

PHIL   I don't.

WES   It's killing us, man. Capitalism. Killing our kids.

DINO   Have you been reading those Buddhism books on
           the toilet again?

           (LEONIE *laughs*.)

WES   Well, what makes you happy? Phil? Your car?
           Your chest freezer? Kate Moss's tit-less new
           fragrance?

PHIL   My kids.

WES   Och! Kids!

PHIL   It's the smell of them when they've just got in to
           bed. All milky and . . .

WES   Leonie?

PHIL   . . . fresh.

LEONIE   Does Diet Coke count?

WES   No. Dino?

DINO   My job.

WES   Really happy?

DINO   My job. The words. Using words to sell things. I
           love it.

WES   Apart from your stupid job?

DINO   Well, then . . . Suzi. My Suzi makes me happy.

WES   Yeah? More than being on your own? More than that simplicity? And that solitude? And that peace?

DINO   Yes. She makes me happy. Seeing her face first thing in the morning. Warm and soft and calm.

WES   Well, wait 'til you have kids, pal. And that face looks tired and fed up and like it could kill you for not getting up in the night as many times as she did. And for getting her pregnant in the first fucking place. And for even thinking of having sex with her now! Or ever again!

DINO   Well, maybe I'll never see that look . . .

WES   (*not picking up on it*) Huh! You will! Once you have kids.

DINO   Maybe I won't have kids though.

WES   You will! Of course you will! You're always saying how much you want them.

DINO   It's not always that simple though, is it?

WES   If she doesn't do it for you anymore, think about Kelly Brook! I do.

DINO   Jesus!

LEONIE   Please, Dino! Anyway, I don't think we're doing such a bad thing. In this industry.

WES   No?

LEONIE   We haven't killed anyone.

WES   Haven't we?

LEONIE   I haven't.

WES   What about that poor wee boy who's got stabbed for his iPod? You've got to have an iPod. That's what we tell people. You can't be happy – or cool – without a thousand of your favourite, stupid songs on your fat hip. So, when that kid with the iPod is killed by a kid who hasn't got an iPod and can't afford an iPod and can't even spell bleedin' iPod – haven't *we* killed him?

LEONIE   I didn't do an iPod campaign.

WES   The industry!

DINO   It was a good campaign, that! Market share was up eleven percent!

WES   Just a shame about the dead kid!

PHIL   (*to* LEONIE) How's your dog's mange?

LEONIE   Oh, much better, thanks. Yeah. Fancy you remembering my little Baby Boy. He's off the antibiotics now but he still looks a bit scrawny so I leave him at home. I'll be taking him everywhere again when he's looking all nice and fluffy. (LEONIE's *phone goes.*) Oh, hi, Katie!

DINO   And we haven't made people fat.

WES   Of course we have.

DINO   We've only given them more choice.

WES   Choice! Choice just fucking confuses people!

DINO   We tell them what's out there.

LEONIE   Yeah?

DINO   It's up to them what they buy. What they eat. What they believe.

WES   They believe what we tell them. Otherwise we wouldn't be here now. And they believe us

because they're stupid. And they're stupid
because we've replaced the age-old goal of the
acquisition of knowledge with the new goal of the
acquisition of shite. You. And me. And her. And
him. And him. And her – beautiful Amanda –
wherever she's floated off to.

DINO   You need a coffee.

WES   (*his face, drunkenly, far too close to* DINO'S) You
            need to clean your teeth!

PHIL   I've got a cure for the obesity thing.

LEONIE   Okay.

            (DINO *tries to smell his own breath.*)

PHIL   When people get above sixteen stone, feed them
            to the poor.

WES   Jesus! Oops!

DINO   You're okay. She's not listening!

LEONIE   That's great!

WES   Good idea though, Philip! You'd potentially say
            'goodbye' to obesity and world hunger at the
            same time!

PHIL   It's not technically my idea; it's based on an
            essay by Alexander Pope.

LEONIE   Wicked!

DINO   Yes. Pope. Of course.

LEONIE   Bye! (*She ends the call.*) That's Sean Bean
            confirmed for 'Homepride' for tomorrow . . .

PHIL   Better wear some 'Huggies'.

            (JULIAN *waves.* PHIL *presses the talkback.*)

JULIAN	Was that the client?
PHIL	Still waiting, matey. Sorry.
	(AMANDA *returns from the loo.*)
AMANDA	Any news?
PHIL	Still waiting, Amanda. Sorry.
WES	(*OTT*) Sorry!
	(PHIL *takes his finger off the talkback.*)
WES	Lovely Amanda! Look at her!
LEONIE	Or maybe don't!
WES	What about you and Sean Bean?
LEONIE	I'm not married!
WES	Well, aren't you the lucky one?
AMANDA	Tess Daly's still out there.
JULIAN	Did she spot you?
AMANDA	She raised her eyebrows.
JULIAN	Terrifying!
AMANDA	It went right through me.
JULIAN	You know if I was Vernon Kay, I think I'd have to have Tess . . . daily.
AMANDA	(*generously*) You've still got it!
PHIL	You know what I think's weird about this business though?
WES	Tell us, O Wise One!

PHIL   We barely sell anything tangible any more. It's all
              e-this and i-that. And Wii-this and why-that. We
              hardly sell anything that actually exists.

WES   Apart from bleedin' cars!

PHIL   Bananas. We don't do any adverts for bananas.
              'Get your lovely, bananas. Only 90p a pound at
              Tommy's market stall. They're really lovely! And
              yellow!'

WES   Maybe we're not so shite after all!

DINO   Where's bloody Jenny?!

              (DINO *marches to the fruit bowl.* LEONIE *looks at
              her phone.*)

JULIAN   We could try again, you know.

AMANDA   Don't be ridiculous! We went wrong
                    long before we went wrong.

JULIAN   We could still do it. Undo what we did.

AMANDA   Jules! You don't even know me any
                    more.

JULIAN   We know each other better than
                    anyone. People don't change; they
                    just get more bitter.

AMANDA   That's not exactly a hard sell.

WES   Chuck us that magazine.

DINO   If it keeps you quiet.

WES   You love me really!

DINO   Do I?

              (DINO *hands him a magazine.*)

JULIAN   So, what went wrong with Stephen
                Slaney?

AMANDA   What?

(WES *reads from the front of the magazine.*)

WES   Stephen Slaney! Look at him! Ever noticed how
        every word in the English language beginning with
        'sl' has a negative connotation?

AMANDA   What?

DINO   What?

WES   Think about it – (*Pointing at the magazine.*) – Sly.
        Sleazy. Sluggish . . . Slaney.

JULIAN   What went wrong with Stephen
                Slaney?

PHIL   Slag.

JULIAN   The press were saying it was a
                'marriage made in heaven'.

WES   Slug.

JULIAN   That you were 'the perfect couple . . .'

AMANDA   I'm not going into all that now.

WES   Slap. Slip. Slovenly.

JULIAN   We've gone into everything else.

WES   Slapper, slurp.

AMANDA   Okay. I wanted to have children and
                he didn't.

WES   Slippery.

AMANDA		Wouldn't.
JULIAN		Ha!
AMANDA		Irony of ironies.
LEONIE	Slushy.	
AMANDA		Don't say a word.
DINO	Slough.	
JULIAN		I wasn't going to. I don't know if I can have children now.
AMANDA		Biologically?
DINO	Slack.	
JULIAN		No. Psychologically.
AMANDA		What?
JULIAN		The child I should have had, I didn't have. We didn't have.
LEONIE	Slapdash.	
JULIAN		So, how will I be able to look at a child now, my child, without thinking it's the wrong one. It shouldn't look like this – it should look like 'her'. Like me and you.
AMANDA		Jesus Christ, Julian!
JULIAN		I should want a child. I should want to continue the line but there's a beat missing. Our beat.
PHIL	Sliver.	
JULIAN		No one tells you at the time. You talk about it, the rights and wrongs, the

	pros and cons. You make the call, they take your money, do the necessary and send you home.
PHIL	Slipshod.
JULIAN	No one says 'You do know this will stay with you, somewhere in your soul, for the rest of your life?' It's not supposed to. I'm the man. It wasn't my body after all.
LEONIE	Sleeve.
WES	A sleeve isn't negative.
LEONIE	It is on a vest.
AMANDA	You seemed fine at the time.
JULIAN	I was. I suppose.
AMANDA	Better than me. Much better.
JULIAN	But now there's a gap where there should be something. Every time I've been with friends with children recently, I've felt this gap next to me.
WES	Slash!

(WES *gets up and goes off to the toilet.*)

LEONIE	Sloshed?
DINO	And disillusioned.
LEONIE	That's not a 'sl' word.
DINO	I think we've finished that now.
AMANDA	Well, I'm really sorry you have that gap now, Jules.

PHIL   There's nothing more painful for a man than
              disillusion.

AMANDA   Really sorry.

PHIL   Apart from going to the hygienist maybe.

AMANDA   But I've had that gap at some point
                              every day for eight years. Every day.

              (DINO *sniffs his own breath again.*)

PHIL   Slipping out too . . . (*He leaves the room.*)

AMANDA   So, just because you suddenly feel
                              guilty, or whatever it is you're
                              suddenly feeling, are we all supposed
                              to feel sorry for you? Tell you it was
                              wrong? Turn back time? It hasn't
                              gone away for me – ever.

LEONIE   (*to* DINO) What's going on with you two today?

DINO   I had a conversation with someone at the awards
              last night.

LEONIE   Who?

DINO   Andrew House. From *House, House, Buchanan,
              House and House.*

LEONIE   They want you to go there?

DINO   Next week.

AMANDA   And a child wouldn't necessarily
                              have kept us together. It, she, he
                              could just as easily have driven us
                              apart.

LEONIE   But don't you come as a pair?

AMANDA   And then what? The child sees us
                              rowing, miserable, separating, spends

	weekends here, weekends there. All that?
DINO	He doesn't care about this now. About the work. About 'us'. Not anymore.
LEONIE	He's just tired. He was telling me last night.
JULIAN	She might have brought us together.
LEONIE	I think.
JULIAN	A child now could.
LEONIE	A six-year old and a two-year old. And he doesn't get anything from being a Dad.
JULIAN	She'd fill that gap.
AMANDA	Children shouldn't just be about filling gaps, Jules.
LEONIE	He feels like his life has gone.
DINO	Well that doesn't really help me.
JULIAN	But you can't know it was right.
AMANDA	It was right.
JULIAN	Why was it right?
LEONIE	It's only a job!
JULIAN	Why was it right?
AMANDA	Because maybe I just didn't love you enough, okay? Maybe I just didn't love you enough to have your baby.
JULIAN	But we'll never know.
AMANDA	(*kindly*) No. We'll never know.

DINO	When you find out you can't have kids, your work suddenly becomes even more important.
AMANDA	We only have this.
DINO	And to see someone who's got what you want, what you desperately want, not happy with it, it makes you dislike them even more.
LEONIE	I can't ever imagine wanting to have kids. The whole thing terrifies me.
AMANDA	Look, Jules, it might look like I've got everything but I can tell you this . . .
LEONIE	All that mess; all that responsibility. All that yogurt.
AMANDA	. . . More than anyone else I can tell you.
LEONIE	Now we've got choice, I don't know why anyone would choose to have kids.
AMANDA	The other day, I sat down to make a will. And I realised, I had no one to leave anything to. Without that what's the point, really?
LEONIE	I mean, if it's all about fear of mortality, we're all immortal now anyway.
DINO	Because 'we've found God'?
LEONIE	Because of YouTube.
AMANDA	What's the point?
DINO	I didn't think I wanted them. You see people change so much. Friends becoming parents. They disappear.
JULIAN	Do you regret it?

AMANDA   I don't know.

DINO   I don't know why I'm telling you this but when
              you find out you can't, you *actually* can't, some
              small thing inside you just dies.

AMANDA   In a way. Yes.

LEONIE   But if it's what God wants for you.

AMANDA   In a way I do.

DINO   What?

LEONIE   If that's what God wants for you . . .

DINO   Leonie?

LEONIE   Yeah?

DINO   I'm really glad your faith helps you . . .

              (LEONIE's *phone goes.*)

LEONIE   Sorry. (*Into phone.*) Hello, Jenny.

DINO   (*knowing she won't hear*) But it's fuck all use to
              me.

              (WES *returns from the toilet.* PHIL *behind him.*)

WES   (*arms aloft*) Slogan! The sloppiest, sleaziest,
              slyest 'sl' of all!

LEONIE   No, that's fine. We've been sitting here polishing
              away, Jenny, so . . .

              (JULIAN *has spotted* LEONIE *on the phone.* LEONIE
              makes a thumbs-up gesture to the booth. WES
              slumps onto the sofa.)

JULIAN   (*nodding to the booth*) Looks like
                          this is it, then.

WES   (*projecting*) Hi, Jenny!

LEONIE   Shh! (*To* PHIL.) What's the best way to do this?

PHIL   Hold the phone to the speaker.

LEONIE   No, other clever, technical stuff?

PHIL   Umm . . . nope!

WES   (*projecting*) I love you, Jenny! With your cute, little, high-powered arse!

DINO   Shut up, Wes!

WES   Oh! What am I? Your child?

DINO   Shut up!

LEONIE   (*she nods to* PHIL) Here it is!

WES   Your little baby?

           (*The ad is played to the client.* DINO *grabs* WES *by the throat.*)

AMANDA   *WE'VE GONE TOO FAR!*

JULIAN   *WE HAVE* NOT *GONE TOO FAR!*

           (DINO *grapples with* WES.)

AMANDA   *WE HAVE! LOOK!*

JULIAN   *IT'S THE NEXT LEFT.*

AMANDA   *SO, YOU KNOW MORE THAN THE MAP?*

DINO   You drunk twat!

JULIAN   *PERHAPS THERE'S A MISTAKE ON IT.*

AMANDA   *YEAH, THEY PROBABLY DELIBERATELY PUT MISTAKES ON MAPS TO MAKE DRIVING MORE EXCITING!*

WES   That's a great line!

           (JULIAN *GRUNTS.*)

DINO   Get off me!

AMANDA   *EXCUSE ME, WHICH WAY IS BLOCKLEY ROAD?*

JULIAN   (*RURAL ACCENT*) *OH, YOU'VE GONE WAY PAST IT, LOVE.*
           IT'S . . .

AMANDA   *THAT'S ALL I WANTED TO KNOW . . .*

JULIAN   *STOP GLOATING!*

AMANDA   *I AM NOT GLOATING.*

JULIAN   *YES, YOU ARE.*

AMANDA   *NO, I'M NOT.*

WES   Come on, then!

JULIAN   (*VOICE-OVER-VOICE*) *THE NEW VM VOGEL HAS SAT-NAV*
           FITTED AS STANDARD. IT GETS YOU THERE – NO
           ARGUMENT!

           (LEONIE *takes the phone from the speaker and*
           puts it back to her ear. WES *breaks away from*
           DINO *and slouches down into the sofa.*)

WES   Fuck off!

DINO   You fuck off!

           (PHIL *picks up his mobile and switches it on.*)

LEONIE   No, that wasn't part of the advert; that was just
           . . . No. Yes. We can do that. Yes. Okay. No. No.
           No. No. Yes. Fantastic. Thanks, Jenny. You sure
           you don't want to hear it again? No, that is nice.
           Yeah, I'll tell them. Bye. She doesn't like it.

WES   Fucking shit-arse wanker!

DINO   Why not?

LEONIE   She just doesn't like the script.

WES   She approved it yesterday!

LEONIE   In essence! It wasn't written remember! She likes the performances. But just doesn't like the script.

WES   Which bits, specifically?

LEONIE   All of it. Except the improv.

DINO   Jesus!

         (WES *grabs the award.*)

WES   Does she know we've got an award? Does she know how good we are? Award-winning fucking writers. We've had sketches on *Tittybangbang*.

DINO   (*to* LEONIE) What do we do?

WES   Twice!

LEONIE   She wants me to put back transmission 'til Friday. So, it means writing something totally new this afternoon. And re-recording tomorrow.

PHIL   (*to himself*) That should be fun.

LEONIE   If the guys are available.

PHIL   I'll put you in the book.

LEONIE   Guys, did you get all that?

JULIAN   Yeah. All of it!

LEONIE   I'm really sorry.

(AMANDA *and* JULIAN *start to pick up their things.*)

DINO   Thanks, Amanda. Thanks Julian. We'll see you tomorrow.

AMANDA   I need to check with the Dickens people . . .

LEONIE   Of course.

WES   Shame. Not your fault. You were great.

AMANDA   Was I okay?

WES   Oh, yes. Great! Beautiful, in fact.

JULIAN   Thanks.

WES   And you were really good together.

DINO   Echo that.

            (*A pause.* LEONIE *turns and begins to pack up her things. Suddenly we hear the noise of a child laughing and laughing again. And again. It is* PHIL's *ringtone.*)

PHIL   Hello? Hello, my little Princess! (*To the gang.*) Sorry. (*To the phone.*) No, Daddy's at the studio. Did you have a nice time at nursery?

WES   (*to* DINO) Pub?

DINO   Yes!!

WES   I've got something to tell you.

DINO   Me too.

WES   What?

DINO   It'll keep.

PHIL   And did she say you were a good girl?

DINO   (*picking up their award*) D'you want this?

WES   Why not. Might as well go out with a bang, eh?

                (WES *and* DINO *pick up their award and their
                things and leave.*)

PHIL   And have you been drawing more of your nice
                pictures?

                (PRESTON *enters.*)

PRESTON   All done?

LEONIE   All done. Laters.

PRESTON   Laters.

                (LEONIE *leaves, waving at* JULIAN *and* AMANDA *and*
                PHIL. PRESTON *follows* LEONIE.)

PHIL   And did they let you bring them home, Princess?

AMANDA   I'd better get to my rehearsal.

JULIAN   And I've got my two o'clock.

PHIL   Shall Daddy see it when he comes home?

JULIAN   See you tomorrow, then? Probably.
                                Possibly.

AMANDA   Bye, Jules.

                (*She starts to leave then turns and hugs him hard.
                Then kisses him on the cheek and goes.*)

PHIL   Daddy'll be home for tea. Yes. We'll put it on the
                fridge.

                (JULIAN *hears* PHIL – *the talkback has been left
                'up'.*)

PHIL   Okay, princess. Yes. Daddy loves you too.

                (JULIAN *leaves the booth.*)

PHIL   Very much. (*Pause.*) Do you want to put Mummy
                on?

                (PHIL *is left alone in the studio. A second's
                silence. The lights snap off.*)